THE ADVERSARY!

Apostle Andrea Lewis

Selah Communications, Inc.

Copyright © 2015 by Apostle Andrea Lewis.

All rights reserved.

No part of this book may be reproduced or transmitted in any form or by any means whatsoever: electronic or mechanical, including photocopying, recording, or by any information storage and retrieval system, etc., without permission in writing from the copyright owner.

All Scriptures are from the KJV.

Selah Communications, Inc.
PO Box 79493
Atlanta, GA 30357

Library of Congress Control Number: 2015911333
ISBN: 978-0-9909449-0-4 (Hardback)
ISBN: 978-0-9909449-1-1 (Paperback)
ISBN: 978-0-9909449-2-8 (E-Book)

10 9 8 7 6 5 4 3 2 **1**

Dedication

Righteous art Thou, O Lord; in Thee do I put my trust. Thou hast made me a sheep in wolf's clothing and hadst hidden me from those that would devour me. They, being afraid, judged me and shunned me and refused to know me. They thought to destroy me but only left me for dead. They did not slay me because I looked like a form of them, but I am not like them; I indeed belong to You and ever did. From the moment You made me and through eternity, I will ever be obedient to You and love You more than my own existence/life.

I am indeed their adversary, as You have made me. They, who hate truth and love lies. They, who profess to love and serve You but do hate You, for they love their own lives more than You. They, who mock and jeer and have no true knowledge of You. They, who in truth, cannot give love because they know it not and love not themselves. They, who rob and scatter Your people using Your name, yet feel no shame neither repent....

I am the adversary of the Lord's enemies, and I stand with Him as His axe and His instrument according to His desire.

Please keep me faithful and obedient. Thank You, Lord.

Thank You also, for the remnant that do see and hear. May these receive all You have prepared for them and come to know You in a better way.

Table of Contents

Acknowledgment 7
Preface 9
Chapter I: Righteousness 13
Chapter II: Sin 21
Chapter III: Confusion 27
Chapter IV: Praise 33
Chapter V: Refuge 39
Chapter VI: Peace 43
Chapter VII: Surrender 49
Chapter VIII: Acknowledge 57
Chapter IX: Hope 63
Chapter X: Trust & Faith 69
Chapter XI: Love 73
Chapter XII: Truth 79
Postface 87
Encouragement 89

Acknowledgment

In Thee, O Lord, do I put my trust: let me never be put to confusion. Deliver me in Thy righteousness, and cause me to escape: incline Thine ear unto me, and save me. Be Thou my strong habitation, whereunto I may continually resort: Thou hast given commandment to save me; for Thou art my rock and my fortress. Deliver me, O my God, out of the hand of the wicked, out of the hand of the unrighteous and cruel man. For Thou art my hope, O Lord God: Thou art my trust from my youth. By Thee have I been holden up from the womb: Thou art He that took me out of my mother's bowels: my praise shall be continually of Thee. I am as a wonder unto many; but Thou art my strong refuge. Let my mouth be filled with Thy praise and with Thy honour all the day. Cast me not off in the time of old age; forsake me not when my strength faileth. For mine enemies speak against me; and they that lay wait for my soul take counsel together, Saying, God hath forsaken him: persecute and take him; for there is none to deliver him. O God, be not far from me: O my God, make haste for my help. Let them be confounded and consumed that are adversaries to my soul; let them be covered with reproach and dishonor that seek my hurt. But I will hope continually, and will yet praise Thee more and more. My mouth shall shew forth Thy righteousness and Thy salvation all the day; for I know not the numbers thereof. I will go in the strength of the Lord God: I will make mention of Thy righteousness, even of Thine only. O God, Thou hast taught me from my youth: and hitherto have I declared Thy wondrous works. Now also when I am old and greyheaded, O God, forsake me not; until I have shewed Thy strength unto this generation, and Thy power to every one that is to come. Thy righteousness also, O God, is very high, who hast done great things: O God, who is like unto Thee! Thou, which hast shewed me great and sore troubles, shalt quicken me again, and shalt bring me up again from the depths of the earth. Thou shalt increase my greatness, and comfort me on every side. I will also praise Thee with the psaltery, even Thy truth, O my God: unto Thee will I sing with the harp, O Thou Holy One of Israel. My lips shall greatly rejoice when I sing unto Thee; and my soul, which Thou hast redeemed. My tongue also shall talk of Thy righteousness all the day long: for they are confounded, for they are brought unto shame, that seek my hurt. - Psalm 71

Preface

Who is it that speaketh? Elohim (The God of Israel).

Truth, Knowledge, Light, Wisdom, Understanding, favor, and blessing is given to the yearning ones. Also, an extended hand is offered to a people beloved of God but know it not.

Examine yourself; is anything missing? Let your approach exceed self and access spirit. What does your spirit long for? It's time to be real with yourself and with God. It's time for Truth, Knowledge, Wisdom, and Understanding. It is time to break down and to build up, to fill up the empty, and to refresh the full. It is also time for those cast off and unloved to know their worth, and to know they have never been separated from the giver of complete love.

THE ADVERSARY!

I
Righteousness

There is only One righteous: Jesus, Who is God. In Him we live; in Him we breathe.

We are required to be like Him. What does that mean exactly? And, can we as humans measure up? The answer to the second question is yes. Through grace and mercy we are counted righteous. Through grace and mercy He covers much, so we may be and remain saved. There is a way prepared for every child of God to walk through. To be counted righteous, everyone must walk along that prepared path in faith and trust following hard after God in obedience. Righteousness is putting God first always. A heart, mind, and spirit that puts God first is counted righteous unto God and is perfect before Him. Being counted righteous and seen as perfect by Him is us being in the likeness of God; this is what pleases Him; this is what He delights in.

So..., let's break it all down and get real.

Human beings, since the first sin, have been filled with errors and remain so. Adam and Eve were made perfect and righteous as God is perfect and righteous; but He gave them choice and the capacity to sin, just as we are given choice and just as we maintain the capacity to sin.

Sin and evil existed with them as it exists with us, for the fallen did appear and was present in the garden. Being pure and being without the knowledge of sin and evil, they put God first as it ought to be; He fellowshipped with them daily. Then, one day, knowledge of good and evil, and darkness and light entered them, and they didn't put God first. They deliberately and knowingly made the wrong choice to disobey God; that disobedience was the first sin (in Earth; the power of darkness, evil, and sin being introduced and activated in what was created pure and good). So, they received just punishment, and mankind carried it till Christ came. The deliverance and salvation Christ gave us at the cost of His life and blood is the enabling of all mankind to be counted righteous if we choose Him and put Him first. We will never be so pure as to be free from errors; we can never be righteous (only God is righteous), but through and by the blood of Christ we are counted so in His eyes.

Mankind was made having choice.

What does that mean concerning God? It is simply the knowledge of choosing good, the capability of making errors, and the capacity to sin.

Why did He make us so? He made us so because He wants all mankind to choose Him willingly. There is life and death, therefore choose life.

This ability of choice carries with it the dark side of errors and sins. If you make the wrong choice you are in error, and if you make a choice against God you are in sin. If any think this was a bad thing for God to do in making us this way, then think then of yourselves.

Which of you would be pleased with someone being forced to love you or being forced to be with you?

Would you feel treasured, loved, and wanted?

Would their professed love be sincere?

Do you not want someone who willingly chooses you?
If you find only this willing kind of love good enough for you, what say God?

When made, Adam and Eve were perfect and righteous as God because their capability of errors was not yet activated. They were indeed entirely pure, and not just counted so, because they had not yet made any wrong choice in their entire existence. Though pure in choice and action, they had in them the capability of error and capacity to sin which they did fall to afterward. When they received that temptation within themselves and let it find a place of rest in them, they were in error for the very first time. This activated the capability of errors and capacity to sin within them and for all mankind after them; both they and all under their dominion was also cursed. Thus, discord was and is ever present in mankind and in this whole world (nature, atmosphere, earth, land, seas, waters, beasts, animals, birds, etc.) and will not cease until **all** mankind returns to God. So indeed, an error activated errors, and sin activated sins.

Since that first error mankind has been full of errors, and since that first sin mankind has been prone to sins. We can only be counted or seen as perfect through Christ's blood and through His eyes of love. Before Christ came, God saw Abraham and others through His eyes of love which also searched their hearts. He knew that their hearts chose Him, loved Him, believed Him, and put Him first. As a virgin cannot regain his or her virginity after that first time, though they may choose to abstain for the rest of their years, in this same way, mankind is no longer righteous. This is so because the choice to embrace error and to embrace sin, knowingly or unknowingly, is activated in us and in this world. So, *being good and doing good* doesn't and cannot make us righteous and pure, only God in His mercy and grace can. He sees past our errors and cleanses our sins when we put Him first and when our hearts choose Him. Then, because of love and respect for Him, we are (try to be) good and do good. Again, He blesses us more because the good that we are and that we do is *not for any self-gain* but is *a* **result** *of the love and respect we feel* for Him, for all others, and for all else. Viewing us through Christ's blood and through His eyes of love, He sees us as though we are pure, He sees us as though we are righteous, and He sees us as though we are perfect.

We hear the saying repeatedly, "Only God is perfect; only God is righteous," and the reason for this saying and this truth is the great difference between God and man. The reason is, unlike us, God is an ever/eternal existing being without the choice of errors in Him and without the capacity to sin. He can never make errors because there is no choice nor capability in Him to do so. He can never sin because He doesn't contain that capacity to do so. He can never be tempted because to receive temptation within is an erroneous act. Though Christ went through temptation, He cast down each one and was not affected. He reminded the tempter: it is written *thou shalt not tempt the Lord thy God*. **God and Christ is** *all pure* **and** *all righteous* **and** *all good*. So, since there are no errors nor choice of errors in God, every thing He made and everything He does is exactly how it was meant to be for His glory. There is purpose to everything He does and says, always.

[Christ said, **"Why callest thou Me good? There is none good but** *one, that is, God."* *This was said to one that approached Him and called Him good Master; seeking what thing he shall do to gain eternal life. Jesus answered rightly so because this one was not aware of Christ's Godly/divine nature. He looked on Christ not as God in flesh nor sent by the Father out of Heaven but as a man. So indeed Christ's answer was truth; hoping this one would see that there is no man that is good; revealing that neither could that one do anything good to receive eternal life. If that one looked at Christ as the Son of God, then Christ would not have responded in such a manner. If that one looked at Christ for whom Christ was he may not have needed to ask such a question, for he would know the way to eternal life was not through good deeds but to follow Christ. He looked at Christ as an earthly man, so why call Him good? There was no reason to call Him good because there is none good. Christ was also teaching that there was nothing that one who approached could do himself to be good in order to receive life. Christ instructed him toward love and respect and to follow God, but that one went away sad fearing the loss of his possessions because he did not see God, so he did not receive Him. He saw Christ as a man, so he went away empty and without life.]*

Christ, who was God in flesh, did contain the capability of errors and the capacity to sin just as we do (all human beings are made/born this way), but His Spirit within was holy. He put His Father first always. He remained righteous, mastering and ruling the flesh that can be weak and unwilling. He cast off Satan's temptations in order that He would be that pure sacrifice unto the Father for us, so we may live and be counted pure before God. He also remained pure to show us how to walk, teaching that being faithful and obedient can be done, despite all our negative (undesirable and unwelcome) capabilities and capacities. He showed also that in times of weakness turning to the Father will cause us to receive the strength we need.

How do we put God first? How do we choose Him? Mankind will make many errors till the end of time, even those who endeavor to live for God, because the capability is ever active in us. It is never for us to consistently embrace these errors without fault because we are responsible for our choices; neither is it for us to stay in errors feeling helpless to rise from them because we can recover from them. The Spirit of God is in all who receive Him, aiding us to make correct choices and giving us strength to recover. Your relationship with God is a love relationship. When you realize this fact and live in this way, you will make much fewer errors. You will commit fewer sins. You will live up to your potential. You will be more beautiful on the inside. You will be as perfect in His eyes. You will be as righteous before Him and be as pure in Him, etc. He loves us all deeply and wants to be everything to us that we allow Him and trust Him to be. Embrace Him by believing and knowing that His love for you is true and real; you will then find yourself thinking of Him more and more and beginning to love Him back.

Now, how do you behave in a love relationship that is not fleeting but real and true? There is not much difference in a true relationship with God than with your mate. There should not be **any** day, from the time you wake until the time you go to sleep, that you don't think of Him a lot or at least once; you may even dream of Him from time to time. Your dreams are often the opportunities He uses to speak to you because that is when you are most quiet or still and able to listen. Also, that time is mostly when self, insecurities, and hindrances are out of the way. Never ignore a dream that feels uncommon, especially if it is a dream that you receive repeatedly. It is a warning, a promise, something you need to attend to, or things and ways you need to change. It is your God speaking. He is righteous and just; He is a God who does not speak without purpose, so listen and attend to Him. As you live through your day, know that the choices you make will always affect your relationship with Him in a good way or a bad way. So, as you would behave in your relationship with your mate, you try to choose the things that would please Him.

In this true love relationship, honesty and sincerity is required. You think of Him before you think of yourself. You make the choices that will improve your relationship and draw you closer together. So now you wonder, how do I do that? You simply behave in love and act in love. He is pure and righteous and has extended Himself to you, so He is never out of your reach. There is nothing hidden from Him; He is the best friend you can have; there is *nothing* that you can't talk to Him about. He is interested in every aspect of you and your life. He loves you; He made you; He fights for you; turn to Him; He will help.

Talk to Him about everything. Talk to Him about life, love, sex, money, and relationships. Talk to Him about your desires, your wants, your needs, your faults, and your fears. Talk to Him about that neighbor or person at work. Talk to Him about your cheating mate, your selfish mate, your inadequacies, your job, your purpose, your children, your family, and your friends. Talk to Him about your likes, dislikes, and everything else in your life that affect you.

He will do many works in your life.

Do you want to be a better lover to your mate? Talk to Him; He will open your eyes, mind, and heart to see your mate and whisper to your heart the things that will please them.

Do you want to stop being so promiscuous? Talk to Him; He will give you a mind against the misuse of your being and open you to see and address the root of your need as He heals you.

Are you lonely? Talk to Him; He will give you comfort and show you your true purpose. He will put your hands to work in your purpose. He will prepare you in all ways for anyone He has given to share your life.

Are you always angry? Talk to Him; He will open you to see and address the source of that anger. He will teach you forgiveness and give you understanding.

Are you hurting? Talk to Him; He will drive that pain away. He will heal that hurt at its source. Healing may come at an instant or may be a process, depending on the source of that pain and if you are in a situation that needs time.

What is your issue? What ails you? Talk to Him, He cares and is righteous in helping.

Even though He already knows you from beginning to end, when you talk to Him about yourself and your life, and when you show and give Him all your heart, it creates a bond of mutual trust between you both. And, He pulls you closer to Him. In this trust relationship between you, He will show you signs of Himself so you will know He is indeed with you and in your life. He cares.

What is the most personal thing you can think of about yourself? He cares.

What is the most reviling or vile thing you can think of about yourself? He cares.

He will help, whether by giving you knowledge, by equipping you to deal with the experience you must endure, by sending help, or if it takes a supernatural miracle.

Whatever your need, He cares. Maybe, despite your need, your help and blessing is in helping someone else through their situation.

Open yourself to Him; He will show you how He sees you. If there are things you need to change about yourself, He will show you and will guide you in changing them. He will make you a better human being; because, as a *human (post-sin)*, there is always room for improvement. He will make you more effective in your life. If there are things in your life you don't understand, open yourself to Him and He will give you that understanding. If there are things in your life you need to move on from He will give you the strength, courage, and knowledge to do so. Do you need to know if that person in your life is right for you or if you are living the best life possible for you? Ask Him earnestly; He will tell you or show you, but you *must* be willing to hear the truth. If you are unwilling to hear the absolute truth you will only be more confused and in more turmoil because you are unwilling and still cling to your choices.

Also, your unwillingness may cause Him not to answer you because He sees that you are not truly ready to hear and accept the truth. Do not fear; the answer He gives is always best for you because He is righteous and is toward your good. And, it may be that your answer is just what you wanted but your unwillingness and desperation caused you not to hear. So, then you won't be sure you are doing the right thing, or with the right person, or whatever it is; and, how unsettling is that to not be sure? Being unsure in certain things only causes many more errors and may destroy the very thing you were afraid of losing. Be obedient; be faithful. Whatever is good, whatever is love, do that in your relationship with God and your mate and others. This is putting God first, this is accounted righteousness, this is pleasing before Him, and this will bring you more joy and peace in your life and relationships.

II
Sin

When sin enters, what man by himself can resist? There is no strength to withstand it but by God. By Him only will desires to sin perish from within you. Often, deception causes you to feel justified in the thing that has gotten hold of you. Indeed, it does have you in its grip; despite your confidence you do not have control over that sin, or you would not be involved in that thing or be in that company. Something holds you there, and thinking you can handle it is a deception.

What is sin? Sin is disobedience to God. Sin is the thought, feeling, desire, or action, deliberate or unintentional, that is against God and against those who love God. When you foolishly, unintentionally, or unknowingly sin it is a trespass because it was not deliberate; but, though it was not your intent, being unaware doesn't make it any less of an offense. Sin can always be an error though an error is not always sin; but, both are wrong choices with effects, possible punishments, and consequences that others may also have to suffer with you.

This is why the saying, "*karma*," came about from the mouths of those who served other gods, because they were unable to explain their experiences. It is not *karma* nor something the world, nature, or Earth brings about; it is simply the rewards, or punishment and consequences, sent to you from your God above. He is watching all your actions good and bad, and rewards accordingly. Succinctly, He is very displeased at the evil.

These things sent to you are meant to bless you, or to deter you from continuing in your wrong way. They are also your judgment for something very bad, spiteful, or wicked that you have done against Him or to someone that loves Him. This causes the one that loves Him to know that He does love and defend them. Also, that the offender will know He is real, He watches, and that offense will not be tolerated. He is a God that strongly defends those that love Him. He knows whose heart is true toward Him, and who pretends with words or deeds.

Humans, animals, and even wild creatures may patiently allow you to act against them without consequence. But, acting in defense of their little ones, the moment you act against their children or their young, trust that your consequence is issued and will come swiftly. You might just narrowly escape it if you find safety, but trust that it was released to you or unleashed at you.

Likewise, so it is with God in defending those who love Him. You might narrowly escape your judgment if you find safety in God through repenting of the offense. Again, He *will* know if you indeed repented or if it was only soothing words.

Sin is equated with Satan because he became the master/father of sin when he embraced the darkness and allowed it to fill and envelop him. He went from being the most beautiful and full of light, to being so completely filled with darkness that there is no light or life left in him; he is now dead. Since he is a spiritual being, this means that his spirit being is dead (without any hope of eternal life with God), and there is no coming back from that. Though he was in the presence of God and knows the things of Him, the determination Satan made came at a great cost because there is no repentance for him. Though he knows the truth, he is forever lost.

Satan is never to be pitied because he was there with the God we as humans struggled to believe in and struggled to see through faith. Satan saw God face-to-face and was with Him and served Him there in Heaven; he had all we desire, which is to be with God and to see Him. That act of abomination against God did not accomplish what Satan desired. He did not rule in God's stead nor acquired God's Kingdom. Though lost and dead, he is still subject to God and can do nothing unless God allows it.

Lucifer/Satan, being the very first to take such action (sin/embracing darkness), became the father of sin; those who follow in his footsteps, by embracing darkness themselves, are his children. There are some (I pray *very few*), who walk the earth that are dead in spirit as their father and from this they cannot return. Then there are the rest of us (until God steps in), who are lost and used and misled and deceived, and Satan loves to have it so. He loves for us to be in that state because it sets us up to be led down that wrong path, so we may be dead as he is dead. He wants no one to have what he can no longer have, which is life eternal and to share God's Kingdom. Make no mistake, Satan is real; if you allow all light and life to leave your soul you will indeed meet your father and suffer eternally with him. Please..., never make that mistake.

Though Satan and the angels that also embraced darkness with him move about the earth enticing and using many, not all wrong things and sins done are direct influence or acts of Satan and his dark angels. Some things are from the determination in you because you yourself are embracing a form of the darkness. But, he does delight in it all; he encourages it, and emboldens that determination through repeated acts when you allow him in. The darkness is not Satan, he only has fully embraced it himself. It has filled him to maximum capacity and envelops him; he inhabits it and is now the master of all the fallen angels and father of all men who follow that way. He uses any means necessary and allowed to get anyone to follow. The power of darkness is not to be meddled with. It is **deadly** to the well being, life, and soul of **all** who do.

[The darkness spoken of is not the absence of light, nor the darkness that was upon the face of the waters at the time of creation, nor the smoke and clouds God used (at the Mount., in the temple, etc.) to shield His people from experiencing His full glory, which cannot be handled by mortal man.

The darkness spoken of is the same from the beginning, and is the great evil which caused sin and discord in the fallen and in man and all earth. It is the same great evil which Lucifer (who being fallen is now Satan) fully embraced and embodies; the same, which the fallen angels followed after and embraced. This is the same great evil which God desired to protect Adam and Eve from experiencing by giving them that great command not to touch that singular tree. This great evil, which Heaven knew of, was not meant to touch nor mingle with man; man had no knowledge of it and God desired it to remain so. But, the tempter, who embodies it, came and infected them with greed. Man was made to last, had they obeyed, but they did not. So, they died as God said, and still we die, and the earth is destroyed.]

Satan hates for anyone to know who they truly are and the power that is within them, because that puts him at a severe disadvantage with them. Thus, he is less likely to trap them into embracing darkness to the extent that their spirit will be dead as his. Satan embodies darkness (evil) and the fruits of darkness are his weapons; he uses them against mankind in hopes to steal their soul and what he can never have, Glory. Glory belongs to God and will never cease to be so.

The first step Satan uses with people is to deceive them into believing that there is no God or that God doesn't care. This belief removes them or distances them from their help and their refuge against him, making it easier for them to embrace things that are not in their best interest. It leaves them nowhere to turn when he comes against them. When their lifeline of God is removed, or they are made to feel like it is gone, humans feel helpless and hopeless. Then, in steps depression, suicide, and those other feelings and thoughts, causing some to strike out with murders and abominable forms of hatred, also self-hatred; Satan delights in all these things and more.

Still, God allows most of it for reasons and purposes; one great reason is that He will never force or trick anyone to choose Him. Trickery is a tool used for evil; it is making someone choose or believe something untrue to gain their corporation or submission to the thing you desire. No matter what spin you try to put on it, it's purely a selfish act, and there is no selfishness in God. Selfishness is not sin itself but is a great cause of many sins. Selfishness being hand-in-hand with the sin of pride causes many to often fall, and they are both things that God despises.

For some, they think and daydream about many wrongs and evils, but because they have never acted them out they believe they are safe and free from blame. In God's eyes they are just as guilty and filthy as if they did all that they were thinking.

Your thoughts, meditations, desires, and dreams matter; God is watching, God is listening. If they are wrong, God is against them and Satan is pleased with them; if they are good, God is pleased and will add to you, and Satan will dislike all you stand for. So, which of those do you prefer? You choose.

Doing things that are good and right is designed to feel extremely gratifying. Likewise, sin and all wrong feels very satisfying in the person executing that action, indulging in the thought and feeling, or embracing the darkness; since Adam and Eve we are prone to it. Even the cruelest person, in a moment of honesty, will admit to you that there was a form of pleasure or satisfaction in the release of their evil and in their actions. But, there is *never* any sustained pleasure, nor any joy, nor any peace, nor lasting satisfaction in any of their actions: which are the main and consistent consequences of sins, wrong actions, and thoughts. Another consequence of embracing darkness is they begin to lose good conscience; they always feel justified, and their justification is askew.

If you are at the edge, feeling lost and lonely like you are fading, and like there is no light in you or around you, hold on. The fact that you feel this way speaks that you are not yet fully captured, so hope in God. Only He can pull you out from that pit and fill you with Light, Wisdom, Knowledge, and Understanding, and give you peace.

Draw near to God. Seek Him, and believe in Him; He will fight for you. Talk to Him about yourself. Tell Him about the faults and weaknesses you have noticed. Tell Him all the wrong things in and about you that you honestly desire to change; He will mold you and make you better. One day you will notice that things, which once made you so very angry, don't fill you with wrath anymore. You will notice that people, who caused you great pains, no longer have the same effect on you. You will understand their substance and the truth of why they do the things they do; you see their brokenness.

Maybe you are the broken one, who hurt and wound others with your words and the things you do, ask God to change you and He will; it is a process so don't let go or give up. If you don't know yourself or your weaknesses, ask God. He will remove the covers from your eyes to see all that needs to be changed and will help you to be better and be changed.

When you endeavor to choose God and do what is right in all areas of your life, God cherishes you and will help you in all areas that you need help. The more you choose God and what is right, the more sensitive and attentive you will become. You will know more quickly when you are off your path with God and what is best for your life. You will be free from sin (deliberate sin) and have more self-control because you have embraced God and Christ Jesus, and you are kept by Him. You know that when you fall or stray He is there to receive you once again. You will never be perfect, but you will be a better human being on the path of fulfilling your destiny; confident in the knowledge that you are loved with an eternal love that cannot die.

God is King, He rules over day and night, He rules over darkness (evil) and light (good), He is in full control, and He allows what He will for His purposes. He is just, and He is wise. He is filled with wisdom, knowledge, understanding, and He is good.

Since the moment Adam and Eve by greed uncovered the knowledge, we maintain this knowledge of good and evil till this very day, but we have hope (Jesus Christ). When made, He gave man choice, and He desires that you choose Him; since the beginning it was so, and still, He desires you forevermore.

III
Confusion

There is a way prepared for some that is very rough and made as sin. How can you do some things, or speak things that seem so unlike God? Are they not blasphemous and abominations? Yet, God says, "Walk this way," and "Follow Me." How can a holy God cause you to walk in such a way and yet be with you? A way that is unlike anything you had been taught. A journey (to your destiny) you must tread alone; a way others may not yet understand: one lone human and his God. Very unsure, you walk forward with some apprehension. He needs to prove you (afterward giving you companions). He wants to show you who you are and what He needs of you. Also, He desires to show you who He is in truth: without the things the world added to Him.

Would God take you such a way as this? Yes.

Does not the enemy speak? No.

What the Holy One leads you into, He will lead you in, through, or out of, if it be so, even through the depths of Hell.

There are some sins which must be done (allowed) for the fulfillment of His word, but woe to any who find much pleasure in them. Does prophecy fulfillment give anyone the OK to seek sin? No: then you are following your own way and not God. Which sins are for fulfillment and how will you know? The answer is, you don't go looking for sins to commit nor do you provoke sins against you. In your walk following God you will encounter these things and you must trust Him wholly, if not, it will consume you as it did Judas. If you trust Him wholly, and you are innocent, and the sin is done against you, it will propel you into your destiny as it did Joseph.

Nothing that crosses your path is to be pursued. Only things on your path as you go forward (not backward, nor to the right, or to the left) are to be embraced (submitted to). How will you know the difference? In you He will create a great submission to the thing. Submission is not weakness, neither is weakness submission; it is good to learn the difference. Submission is obedience or willingness. It is giving in to a thing though you have strength and power or choice to resist. Be willing, as one would submit to their marriage because it is good to do so, or as Christ submitted to His path and crucifixion because it was good to do so. Weakness is feeling the inability to resist a thing, as in things of lust, greed, or addictions. In weakness, there is a feeling of desperation and helplessness. In submission, there is a feeling of strength, resolve, focus, and determination. When you willingly submit to God in going, in doing the thing, or in speaking the thing, then grace which is greater than any sin, and mercy which is salvation extended, covers you. If you stay connected with Him there is also a constant cleansing so you may remain saved and acceptable before He that is Perfect.

God indeed treasures an obedient and faithful one.

Many things we hold as sin are not, and many things we do disregardfully are vile before God. There are also things that are not sin and not wrong in general but are wrong for your life and path; God may reprove and even punish you though another may do the same acceptably. It is all about obedience and faithfulness to God in all He calls **you** to. Once you have said yes to Him, He brings you to know who you are and what He expects from you. You are now in covenant with Him, and it is now a violation for you to do anything (sin or not) that is against your new nature (being created new), His nature, and the covenant between you. If you are attentive to Him, you will know what pleases Him for you and what does not. In all this, know, that if you pretend for the world and you know it is not right for **your** life with God, He will bring you to live in shame.

In order that you are not led astray by the enemy, their voices, their dreams, or by your own heart, He will teach you His nature and that there is order in Him. His nature will never drive you to harm yourself, and His nature will not drive you to harm anyone. His nature always focuses on His children and the care of them or the deliverance of them. His nature will protect His children from His enemies by whatever means pleases Him. His nature will reprove and punish His children in order to bring them back to Him, and bring them back to what is good for them. His nature is to love and protect you, even from yourself. These are just a small portion of the nature of God; He will teach you the rest if you belong to Him and are faithful and obedient.

There are many things that will cause confusion in your life and in your faith, but understanding will drive it all away. Are you confused about why you are on earth? Seek God to understand your true purpose. He will speak to you and let you know it in a way that you hear and understand Him. He will also plant the desire and passion for it deep in your heart, even connected with your spirit. You will know just who you are; then, you must be faithful and diligent as He builds you in that. While He builds you, never forget that there is time and order to everything. So, be very patient, trust Him, appreciate the journey, and be good to those you meet along the way.

You may be confused about your relationship. If so, get to understand just who that person really is and you will no longer be unsure. Are they for your best interest? If not, either they don't truly love you or something is in the way of their love for you; communicate with them in a real way and you will have your answer. Are you for their best interest? If not, the same goes for you and your love for them; open up and examine yourself in a real way. If you mean them no good or something is in the way of your love for them, then make the necessary changes within yourself to ensure their best and also your peace of mind. Whatever the relationship, whether romantic, friendship, parent and child, or whatever label your relationship has, the relationship and those involved must be understood if your relationship and bond is to survive and thrive. Otherwise, confusion sets in and causes feelings and actions unbecoming, that are ultimately against what you truly desire for that relationship.

Sometimes confusion leads us into desperation: feeling, saying, and doing things we don't mean, or meaning those things in the moment they are said and done until understanding finds us feeling sorry. Confusion will also lead you to seek ways of escape that are poisonous and deadly to your spirit and a destruction to your relationships. Seek to understand yourself and why you feel those ways; you will find that you respond differently. A part of the process of being whole is understanding yourself. A person who understands whom they are is not easily affected by much and certainly not often taken by surprise. As you begin to understand yourself, you will also notice that you are more forgiving of others, because you now see their humanity as you see your own. So, now you understand them a little bit better than you once did, and this newfound understanding will give you clarity and some peace in living. Also, it is the beginning of better and prosperous relationships and a more centered you.

Confusion with God, Who is your lifeline, is the most tumultuous and loneliest experience to pass through; some people don't make it out. It is filled with such heartbreak and uncertainty and insecurity. Wanting desperately to do what is right and being unsure of what exactly that right thing is. Knowing you need to move but feeling stuck and afraid. Knowing what He said, but confusion says, **Was that Him or your own wrong desire?** Accepting truth while needing confirmation and affirmation to truly know, but there is none to give it, because only you believed that much and He trusted only you with such knowledge or with that task or duty. You turn to Him again, knowing or believing He is displeased or angry because you are not obedient to do the things you should; things which you are afraid is wrong because you are confused. Now you are even more confused, understanding nothing. You wonder if He is displeased because you didn't do a right **thing**, or because you thought to do this **thing** which was not good.

Now things are breaking loose in your life, and you are losing things because you are in error; you are so full you can't think. You are very desperate and know you need to move, but you don't know the right step to make and are terrified it will be the wrong move. Suffering situations and feelings that make you want to let go and give up. You stand in a place of error. All you want to do is fix it, and all you want to do is what's right. All you want to do is get out of this place of error, but you don't know how, or don't trust that what you believe you should do is right and pleasing to Him.

He is waiting.

This is time to breathe then step out on faith and act. Do that first thing you were told or felt deep down, because that is truth, that is the right thing, and that is the good thing. This was and is the right step, before fear, doubt, and insecurities came in and clouded your path with confusion. Setting your heart to take that step will set you back on your path with God, even before you take that actual step, because He sees and knows the determination of your heart. This step frees you from that inner turmoil and bondage. It frees you from the terror you felt, that your enemy delighted in. This step gets you back to faith, and faith leads you back to understanding, and understanding leads you back to knowing what is true; back to trusting Him, back to knowing Him, and back in obedience to Him.

So, back to the beginning.... In your journey, on your prepared path, you may have much difficulty. Many others may not understand the steps you take, but trust God; all is necessary to build you in the promise. Remember, though unlike you He was without sin, He too was misunderstood and numbered with sinners, but He was faithful. The charge He has given you is greater than others know and more than others can understand. They don't believe God has anything to do with it because He has revealed more of Himself to you than they can handle.

Many others carry a form of Him with no power. They mock, whisper, stare, laugh at you with others, talk ill about you, and roll their eyes when you speak. They look for you to fail, or worse: they look for you to stay **exactly** where you are. Their eyes are blind and their ears are deaf to the greatness of God and the greatness that is within you. So, they hold no regard for you, and some never will; even some that are close to you will never see. Remember Christ: even after His greatness was revealed, and after all His great works, and after He entered into His glory, there were some, to their shame, that still disregarded Him. They held Him as nothing, and as less than who He truly was and is.

At times even you may wonder about your greatness, because it feels like you are being destroyed. You feel the hatred, betrayal, and neglect from others so strongly. You feel like He is deliberately breaking you; still, He continues to speak love to you. Soon, you'll come to realize He is only taking you through a process that will build your character and your nature, which is necessary as one of His chosen. He also uses these moments to show you Himself, that you may truly know Him.

In your journey, there are or will be things done by you, against you, or both, that though wrong are necessary for your journey and can be no other way. He has or will harden their hearts, your heart, or all hearts; He allowed it or will allow it and bring you through under grace and mercy.

During your season of building, pay close attention to those who are true to you, those who believe with you, and those who believe for you. Remember those who believed and were available to you in the moments when it mattered, and those who accepted you as you were. Remember those who accepted you in your raw state, yet saw the beauty and strength in you. Remember those who saw something in you they couldn't quite put their finger on but knew they had to be good to you and obey God concerning you. Remember those that knew or believed it was all possible for you and genuinely encouraged you in some way. Compile a list if you must, and never leave those ones forgotten; pray for them also, because standing by you may have cost them. There may be or may have been battles in their lives spiritually and naturally because they stood with you, or helped, or believed with you. There may be trouble breaking loose in their lives and they don't understand why, but you understand perfectly with the discernment God gave you. Therefore, you must now intercede in prayer for them so that they will live in victory.

As for the ones who mocked and ridiculed and did acts of wickedness against you, forgive all, and pray for those the Spirit leads you to pray for. It is not good for you to be angry with those who are ignorant of the truth, only pray for them, that they may be opened as you were opened.

The sum of it all is: confusion is bred from a lack of understanding. Seek God for understanding of all things necessary for your journey; in all things you fail to understand, trust God with all your might. Communicate in a real and true way with those in and along your journey so that you may get to understand them and be able to live a better life that affects others in a good way. Seek to understand yourself and know who you truly are, good and bad. Also, examine yourself and learn why you do the things you do, so you can be the better human being God called you to be, and live a life of peace, fulfillment, and clarity.

IV
Praise

*P*raise. Hallelujah anyhow; hallelujah when all is well, and hallelujah when nothing is evident. Hallelujah when your heart is filled with pain and breaking, and hallelujah when your heart is filled with joy. Praise, when God unfolds the things promised in your life; praise, when you are still in waiting. There is praise in an obedient action, and there is praise in remembering just who you are. Praise when you feel ill, and praise when you feel well. Praising when you are in waiting speaks to all others that your love for Him is unconditional; praising when you have received acknowledges and testifies of Him. Praise.

Whatever your circumstance, God has it under control. Be not weary, He will fight your battles and bring you through to your unyielded praise (That great praise deep down inside you that you didn't know existed, until He uncovered it, and had you give it to Him). In this great praise is where God's glory lies, and when it is released to Him, His glory is expanded exceedingly. Praise daily, and praise in the moment; with each breath you breathe, live praise. It is an acknowledgment and an understanding: knowing who you are, and to whom you belong. It is showing and expressing your love, admiration, and acknowledgment to the One you love. It is releasing the respect and gratitude you feel so passionately.

'How do you feel about Me?"

'You are the deepest love I have ever felt and known. I'm unable to breathe (function well) and live outside of You. You challenge me, You test me, You reprove me, You comfort me, You rescue and save me, and You shield me. You prevent me, You order my steps, You provide for me, You remove my pain, You heal my hurt, You lead and guide me;

and, You give me wisdom, knowledge, and understanding. You protect me, You are so good to me, You heal my body and my mind, You show me just who I am, You show me who You are, and You make me feel complete/whole. You give me love, You give me deep comfort, You give me peace, You give me hope, and You give me rest. I am very sad at the thought of You ever leaving me. I feel lost at times when I don't feel You, and I hate it when I make You angry or displeased; I want to stay in line with You always. I want to be obedient to You always. I never want to take You for granted; I always want to give You the respect due You no matter how close You draw me to You. I want to know You and what is good, so well, that my actions and thoughts automatically line up with Your desire and plan for me. I want to never fail You. I want to never give up; I want to never let go; I want to never turn my back; I want to always live in Your promise and be faithful and dutiful to them. I love You, I adore You, I appreciate You, I need You, I want You in my life always, and I want You as head of my life always. I want You to continue to love me, and reprove me, and guide me, and counsel me, and keep me. I want You to never let me go. I want You to keep me bent to You, that I will never go away nor stay away from You, but always return and remain with You where I belong. I thank You for Your protection throughout my entire life; I thank You for the things You have kept me from and the things I experienced. I thank You for all the lessons learned and for Your patience in teaching me. You are my rock and my strength. Without You, I would have perished a very long time ago. Thank You for letting me see You in every thing You did and are doing. Thank You for grace, and thank You for mercy. Thank You for knowing and doing all that was and is necessary to mold me into who I am and is called to be. Thank You for being my God. Thank You for opening me to see, to hear, and to know. You amaze me in the things You speak and the things You do. When I should know and not be so in awe, yet still, I marvel at the things You showed me and said when I see them before me. Though You have given me so much already, still, I want so much more of You. Is it greed or does my passion for You know no end? Yet, please never allow me to seek more than I can handle, but help me to know steps and order and to walk in harmony with You. My entire life belongs to You for Your glory; all my gifts and talents You gave I present before You; may I always be pleasing in Your sight, and may I always remain faithful and obedient, come what may. Many things have I passed through; many more things await me on this Your chosen path for me: some things I will love, and some things I will verily dislike; may I take every step as You designed when You thought of and made me. Please continue to teach me about myself and continue to refine me. Please don't ever hide Your face from me, and please keep me from anything that would cause You to do so. The ways You provide and make for me astounds me, and I am so grateful. You are my light; please continue to shine on me and my prepared path. You make me smile. Thank You for the love and care You made in me for all things. Thank You for my household. Thank You for my family. Thank You for trusting me. Thank You for being my friend and all else You are to me; thank You for making me Your friend, keep me true. I don't understand why You love me like You do, but I thank You for showing me such love and care. Thank You for holding on to me. Thank You for being present in every loneliness; I appreciate You. Thank You for every time You embraced me: filling and surrounding me with such love and peace. For every time You came to me, and every time You allowed me to see You, and every time You allowed me to touch You, thank You. An understanding and a way between friends; something I cannot explain that others would understand, except maybe those whom You have allowed the same; my wondrous Friend. Thank You for making me truly free. Thank You for the well of forgiveness extended to me. Thank You for Your compassion for me. Thank You for knowing me better than I know myself. I am sad whenever I don't know You like You know I should, or like You expect that I would; though I do indeed know You: somewhere deep in me it guides me. Let me never forget You and all You are, I would rather not breathe. Thank You for making me like You. Thank You for truth. Thank You for Your hand extended to me. Thank You for fighting for me. Thank You for Your angels and all the ways they serve You on my behalf. Thank You for my Elite Guardians. Thank You for all the obedient people You sent and brought to my path. Thank You for my faith in You. I love how You love me, and I love how I love You, thank You. You are everything to me, and I am Yours, forevermore."

"I close my eyes in penitent prayer to remember Thee."

'And when I looked upon your face, it amazed Me at how much I love you."

"Amazing grace, how sweet the sound."

You have heard my conversation with Jesus and heard my praise. Yet, it goes so much deeper than you have heard and deeper than even I understand; but, it brings God glory, and this is why I was made. I know not how, nor do I desire, to be any other way now than to live in His praise. I give praises; meanwhile, He inhabits them and draws me in with Him, and this is where my peace lies; this is the place from which my peace is issued; this is the place of my rest. It is my communicative existence with Him, for eternity and through eternity.

Many people praise themselves and praise those around them. This kind of praise has its place and time and is not an evil thing. Nevertheless, if you don't consistently praise God, only acquiescing when told to give praise by the preacher or service leader, you will never learn what true praise really is. Also, you will never access or open up that deep natural reservoir that is inside you.

This praise is almost automatic, and it is a natural part of you; it comes up and flows out of you like a fountain and a fresh spring. It is never forced; it is a mutual and willing communication between you both that sometimes others are privy to hear. It is sometimes quiet within you, and it is sometimes loud and powerful; but, it is consistent and it is constant, even while you sleep. It is not constant because you, in the flesh, stay always praising Him with hands held high and eyes closed, nor does His Spirit stay constantly speaking in heavenly tongues through you. He does not desire nor require this constant physical state of praise from anyone; He made you to live and interact with those around you and to experience life on this earth. Your praise is constant because your spirit now lives in that state of communion with Him: your heart, mind, and spirit is now ever available to Him.

Your whole being is always ready to give to Him and to receive from Him and always ready to act in obedience to Him. You are ever aware of Him, so even when your mouth and body have ceased to praise your spirit does not, and who you are (this new creation) does not. Even in your sleep, your heart, mind, and spirit remain in reverence and connected to Him, and He will from time to time communicate with you there.

Jesus must first visit you and uncover and awaken this recumbent/inactive/dormant praise in which your communication and communion with Him is established and maintained, and He will, in your season.

So, give Him what you have until He comes and opens you to give Him more. Praise.

God be glorified.

V
Refuge

*I*n every good and committed relationship there is a place of refuge, and God is in the midst.

A baby cannot return to the womb; likewise, we cannot return to our sheltered place of preparation.

Once born, the baby may desire that warm, comfortable, and stress free environment it once had before being brought into a chilled and bright environment. Nevertheless, the baby was instilled with courage and bravery that it must access to face its challenges and milestones ahead. The baby cries, maybe with some yearning and regret, and there is no choice for that small one but to move forward with the will to survive, and with love it thrives. The young one moves forward meeting every challenge and every milestone. The babe endures every growing pain one step at a time with courage. Sometimes it is with giggles and sometimes with tears; always learning and growing. Never defeated by failure the little one seeks the way to succeed though at times needing many attempts to master a task, all the while feeling the support of a loved one. A baby cannot hide from those steps it needs to take in learning to walk nor can it run from the pain of those teeth that will grow. All necessary challenges must be faced and overcome so that baby will grow and become the refined adult God intends.

Now with us, in likeness to that newborn, once chosen and birthed into our purpose, we cannot return to the womb of our wilderness or training. There it was hard, but we felt a safety and a comfort that we may now yearn for because there is where we feel we were closest to Him. There is where we were truly hidden and best cared for, where He first showed us who He is, even supernaturally. It was a place and time where we were safe from the harsh world and the terror some people can be, even those who are close to us. However, as the baby, all necessary challenges must be faced and overcome so that we will grow to become the refined and powerful one of purpose as God intends.

God is never that kind of refuge where you run to hide from the world or from pain meet (fit) for you. He will never shield you from living, or from experiences you must endure to mold and refine you, or from those growing pains you must feel. However, as you bravely and courageously take one step at a time, even in tears and shaking off the feelings of regret, you will indeed feel His love and support, and He will heal you of any cuts and bruises. He will also prevent or heal you of any and all infections.

He is the kind of refuge you run to in courage: great courage to face the cruel and unjust, and courage to face the hurt and pain. He is a refuge because He keeps you from emotional and spiritual destruction while you face these things that you must endure to be refined for your purpose. He is a refuge from your emotional suicide and all your self-destructive ways. You cannot use Him to hide from the process of your refining and greatness; He is your refuge to face the terrible and overcome in victory.

Whatever is against you that is not for your refining, He is your refuge that you neither see nor feel it. He will keep you out of your enemy's sight, or cause them to be at peace with you, or cause them to fear even the thought of touching you.

Whatever is against you that is for your refining and for His glory, you will definitely see and feel it, whether small or great. And, because He knows you and trusts you, He will indeed expose your delicate areas to attack. That is why your pain may be so deep, because you were attacked in your sensitive areas and most often by those close to you. But, He is your refuge that you will not be overwhelmed nor defeated.

Though you may be battered and bruised emotionally and spiritually, He will afterwards heal that wound and that pain. Though it may feel like your worst nightmare, know that it could indeed be worst. Know that He will always keep you from feeling the full weight of whatever it is that has come to break you. Regardless, you will feel a surprising sense of calm about you that will cause you to marvel as you say to yourself, 'I'm OK, I'm really OK." You feel the peace (calm, quiet) so thick around you, so thick you feel like you can touch it; you **know** it is God, and that He handled that thing. You actually see God in that moment because His provision in that moment is so clear and tangible.

Others may look at you and mock or say, "Why aren't you troubled, or stressed, or acting like you are in distress?" However, you cannot react as they believe you should because you have a clear vision that sees past the present ordeal. You are not oblivious to it, but you are in your space of peace provided, and you are in your Refuge who instructs you. It is being handled, though they don't yet see.

A parent is a child's refuge, but a parent cannot shield a child from the necessary things needed for growth and development that molds that child into who God made and called that child to be. The parent is a shelter as the child braves the world. They listen, they help, they support, they encourage, they help lessen the pains experienced, they apply medicine that heals the child's wounds, and they give good counsel that heals that child's mind. Many times they also shield that child from gross, harsh, and unnecessary experiences.

A husband, and a wife is each a refuge for their mate.

A good or best friend is a refuge.

A stranger established for your help is a refuge.

A close sibling or a family member close in heart is a refuge.

An animal caretaker is a refuge for that animal or their pet; at times even that pet is a refuge for the owner because they do give help, love, and support, and at times save lives.

Whatever the relationship dynamic, if it be good and nurturing and pure love is in the heart, they are a refuge.

Sometimes you turn to people and things that use you up, trying to fill a space they don't belong. You think you are shielded or saved from what you don't want to feel or accept, but occasionally it tears you; your wound goes deep, but you refuse to forsake this thing you use to hide. Emotionally, if a cold wind blows you feel the shiver to your bones, and if it rains you are drenched and drowning; you hurt daily, you cry, and you feel lost. What do you hold on to so tightly it leaves your fingerprints embedded? Who do you get so lost in that you forget yourself? Is it pills, drugs, or alcohol? Is it sex or someone who has no good use for you? Is it your job or some activity you don't necessarily enjoy? Or, maybe you get lost in **church** and **church things**, feeling no joy, just going through the motions. Didn't hit your vice yet? You know, that thing you use to escape, which doesn't really work and only leaves you feeling worse; you know what it is.

These people and things are not good for you or your spirit, and you are well aware of this in the times when you are alone and reality breaks through. These have not been and cannot be a refuge, they are a form of temporary escape and a trap; they leave you feeling empty. They do not shelter, shield, nor comfort you. A true refuge aids not just your body but your heart, mind, and spirit. A refuge uplifts, strengthens, and supports. It does not contain danger or harm. In refuge there is also peace, courage, good counsel, focus, and direction. It gives you a place to breathe and refresh yourself so you can recover strength to come out swinging and defeat all that came against you.

Finally, Refuge is peace in knowing God is able of all things and will see you through. It is understanding His love for you will never fail to give you the best of His heart for you; therefore, you can rely on Him, and you are indeed secure. With God in your life you can also trust that He will use others in your life to be that physical refuge for you in times of need. He will also use you to be the physical refuge in your loved one's life in their times of need. When you know someone has you shielded and is in your corner, it is much easier for you to step boldly through this world, and easier to face and overcome all its terrors in every form that they come.

Let's break down the word **refuge**.

The syllable **re** indicates *repetition* or setting something back to its original state; **fuge** indicates *driving away*.

So, God never fails to *repeat* this **action** tirelessly, each and every time you need it. What **action** is this? The **action** of *driving away* (in all its meaning) all the things that come to oppress and defeat you (not the things that come to refine you). He causes them to flee and gives you rest from them, leaving you with peace. God will also put all fears to flight. Even that fear inside you that is keeping you from living your life boldly, keeping you from trusting Him with all your heart, and stepping into all He called you to be; He will indeed put that fear to flight. He will set you back into a state of peace and well-being. When you put yourself in His hand, God is your refuge and strength that never ceases and never fails.

VI
Peace

True peace is a blessed gift to calm the hearts, minds, and spirits of all who are faithful to God. Only He can give it, and only He can take it away. If at all you find your peace disturbed, or if you never had it and you need it, look to God because there is no true peace outside of God. When everything around you is crumbling, this gift of peace to you fills you with a magnificent calm and strength that carries you, even when no one on earth expects you to make it.

When you are caught between a rock and a hard place, peace enables you to see the path of escape, or allows you to be still as He needs you to be while He works on your situation. Sometimes when peace comes to you in your situation it may not find you standing. You may only have enough strength to sit still or lie still while peace fills and encompasses you, buffering you from being crushed by all that passes over you and possibly through you. All around you things are failing, and you don't receive the support you need or desire from those close to you. Then, God covers you with peace so you are able to stand, sit, or lie unaffected or unchanged within by what would otherwise destroy you.

In you there is a confidence and a supernatural calm, and you are OK. The lights are off but you are OK. The mortgage or rent is past due but you are OK. You lost all your friends but you are OK. You need a job but you are OK. Your health isn't right but you are OK. Whatever is against you, whether spiritual or natural, whether mental or physical, whether internal or external, whether emotions or otherwise, whoever or whatever it is, you are OK.

God makes you resourceful, and He instructs you in any action you need to take. He makes you OK while He works it out and restores you. Because you trust Him, He will make the way for that roof over your head, and He will give you light to see. Beginning with Himself, He will give you at least one true friend that will never betray you or leave, even when they learn all your dirt. He will give you not just a job but a career and your purpose. And, He will heal your body or keep you till you can get your health right through lifestyle and nutritional changes. What ever it is, He is able and will fix it when you trust Him, and peace will abide in you while He does.

Peace unites your spirit with the will of God for your life. In this connection with Him, your spirit allows your heart and mind to know truth. You know that you don't belong there in your mess, and that it will pass. You also know there is a way out for you, and that good will come to you or be restored in your life. Peace that God gives allow you to see past your present circumstance and know that it will end. Peace is the thing that makes you able to survive things that others don't make it out of.

One writer said, **the peace of God that passes all understanding**, and this saying is true. When others look at you, even when Christians look at you, none understand how or why you are making it. None understand how you are still so pleasant and lovely; they see it's not fake or a cover, and they see it is a genuine thing and confidence emitting from you. Even you. When you see the realities and realize that you truly should not be OK, but you are, or when you look back at what you just came out of, even you don't understand how or why you made it. While you are in it, you can't explain why you are OK, and when you come out of it, you can't explain how you made it; all you can only say is, 'I thank God."

There are only a few who God gives the ability to articulate such things for His glory and a purpose, but all who pass through are His witnesses. Even those who cannot articulate their experiences are His witnesses because others saw them when they were in that mess, and then those same ones saw them out of their mess. They were then able to say, 'I thank God" in the ears of those same ones who didn't believe or looked for the suffering one to fall and perish.

Peace gives you equity with God, in that it enables you to see what He sees for your life and in situations, and to know that which is promised to you *will* be. Peace enacts patience, stillness, and a way of understanding God. Peace fills you with trust for God and His way; your way has failed you and now you have given it to God, and He will work on your behalf. Peace is a keeper of men. It keeps mankind from acting rashly, and it keeps households settled. Despite turmoil around us and in our lives, it keeps our minds, hearts, and spirits from falling prey to our enemies and all that comes against us.

Once God gives it to you, only He can take it away. There are only two known ways for you to lose peace. The first is you can walk away from it, stepping outside of God and His plans for you. This would be because of fear and doubt, or because of a lack of understanding, which causes impatience and confusion in you. But, peace remains with God where you left it, so return to your peace; return to your place in God. The second way to lose peace is if you are so disobedient and reckless, being determined to go your own way, that God removes it from you. In this case, again, you must return to God. But, peace is not so easily found because it was removed, so you must then go through the process of repentance and cleansing before it is restored to you.

The enemy, Satan, and those he uses against you, can never take your peace from you; they can only do what you allow and give them the power to do. You give them the power to rob you when you are disobedient in doing something required by God, also when you believe and embrace the seeds they plant. The seeds are fear, doubt, confusion, disbelief, heightened insecurities, and all the rest they plant to make you step outside of God and away from your peace so they can capture, use, and abuse you. They laugh at you when they see you affected and grieved by your situations, or the situations they caused for you. This is not what God desires for you, that you feel their reproach against you. If you are not in error or deliberately so, and turn from that way, now being obedient, it is the will of God that you walk and live blameless, unashamed, and unaffected. And, He will maintain your peace.

Now, when you are in grave error and your peace is taken from you, if you are clueless that you have repeatedly and consistently done wrong, you will be made aware that your peace is gone. You will be aware when you start to *feel* the hell that has broken loose around you or start to *feel* the hell that has been in your life. You'll feel it because

God Himself gave authority and power allowing those enemies and things to rob you. He made you feel the effects of it in order to turn you from your way back to Him.

Being now affected by it all, you wake up and realize, **Something just ain't right with me or my life**. If the things you have done were not deliberate and knowingly wrong, you will desire to fix it, and this will be the beginning of you turning to Him in repentance. If the things you have done were deliberate and knowingly wrong, or if you were deliberately disobedient by not doing something you knew He required of you, then your pride may cause you to suffer needlessly. You will remain suffering until you are willing to turn back to what is good and right in repentance and submission to Him.

Peace is a precious gift from God and none should ever take it lightly. Nevertheless, some who have it do take it for granted, because He cares so well for them that they lose sight of their source from time to time. It is a great blessing to have peace of heart, mind, and spirit.

Many around you are losing their battle daily, for lack of peace. They cry daily, for lack of peace. Some give up and some reside in misery, for lack of peace. Some take their lives or the lives or others, for lack of peace. Many are lost in the psychiatric system, for lack of peace. There are some who have all the possessions life avails them but are consistently suffering within, for lack of peace. In the church many suffer, for lack of peace. In the world many suffer, for lack of peace. Many pastors suffer, for lack of peace. In leadership some suffer, for lack of peace, also causing those under them to suffer the same. Many homes suffer, for lack of peace, because the head of said household has none. Many employers and employees suffer, for lack of peace. Many love relationships suffer, for lack of peace. Many friendships suffer, for lack of peace. Many parent child relationships suffer, for lack of peace.

Many inflict their misery on all who they can, but so many more individuals go unnoticed suffering greatly in silence, for lack of peace. You cannot always readily tell who is suffering unless God makes you sensitive to such ones; when He does, it is that you may ask of Him on their behalf. You will never know unless you make yourself available by listening to their words and their behavior, then you will see and hear that their peace and hope is disturbed or gone. When you know their lack, it is then your duty to ask of God on their behalf.

When you are blessed with peace in your life, be very grateful. Make a sincere plea or say a sincere prayer for those who don't possess it that they may receive mercy and peace also. God will do what is good and right concerning all people, nevertheless, it is your duty to ask on their behalf when you become aware of their lack of peace. Also, someone may have asked of God on your behalf, so never fail to do likewise.

Peace abides with God and is issued from Him only, so when you feel it don't forget to thank Him.

VII
Surrender

It takes a very strong person to submit. The first vital submission is to your Creator and King. The One Who created you knows best about all things concerning you. Submit to God and His desires for you because His desires are more than you could ever want or imagine for yourself. Your life will be much more fulfilling when you accomplish everything in a manner that is pleasing to Him. Don't resist God; it is best for you to embrace His desires for you; it is best for you to embrace truth, and that path, and the thing your spirit beckons you to accept and to do. Don't resist God; it is best for you to let go of that thing, or that way, or that one, and that thing your spirit cries out against; let Him show you what is best for you. The act of surrendering is always done for the betterment of the situation of the one who surrenders; so, why do we continue to resist?

To submit is not the same as giving up. When you submit, it is to a better way and to accept the authority and knowledge of another. But, when you give up, it is to accept failure and defeat; you were not made to reside in failure and defeat. Never give up on you. We were made to submit to our King, and to submit to each other in love.

There are exceptions in which submission is justified strategy against the enemy. One may yield to unpleasant things for a moment, knowing that it won't last, or while devising a plan of victory over that unpleasant oppressive thing; still, even this is for your betterment because it is for your survival. So, submit to that job for a time, or that situation for a time, or submit to that oppression for a time, until you see the opportunity to escape, then run for your life and never look back. Run to whom you truly are. Apart from those exceptions, never submit to anything that is against who you are, or that is against your purpose and your best interest. Never submit to violence or mistreatment except only to seek a way to escape with your life.

Submit to your husband; submit to your wife; they were created to suit you. Submit to them so they can be to you all that a husband or wife is supposed to be. They have been given authority by God in their respective roles so give yourself to their hand and trust them to do that. God trusts that one with you, so you need to also trust that one, that same one you gave yourself in commitment to. Never withhold yourself from them neither resist them. Never separate yourself from them emotionally nor physically. If you are not yet in a place of trust with your mate then trust God Who trusts them with you. It is your duty as that husband or wife to share yourself (heart, mind, body, and spiritually) with them and not be spiteful nor selfish with yourself concerning them.

Submit, not losing yourself or your identity, but submit being open, accepting, and willing; do not be deliberate nor wicked against them to the detriment of the relationship or their self-worth. You were made to fit each other; you are given to make life easier for each other as a constant source of assistance in every way. Be good to them and trust them to be good to you. It is their duty to be good to you their submitted mate, and it is your duty to be good to them your submitted mate. It is not to submit to any abuse or controlling ways in them but to submit to the love and care a husband or wife is bound to give. Listen to and respect each other's counsel; don't belittle or ridicule each other. One person is not always right. God put wisdom, knowledge, and understanding in both mates, so always yield to what is best for your mate and your relationship, and nurture both.

If you put what is best for the relationship first then you will always be good to your mate, which is in turn good for you also. Submit to the prosperity and the flourishing of your relationship and of your mate; this is the submission God desires and why He said, **submit yourselves one unto the other**. You were made to balance each other; you are each other's help. Whether you are male or female, if you cannot submit, you are not mature enough for relationship and marriage. Wait and let God prepare your heart, mind, and spirit for such commitments and submission, or you may destroy the very thing, and one, you love and desire.

Submit to your mate who is an help meet for you as they submit to you who are an help meet for them. To submit is not weakness, it is strength of character: knowing, admitting, and accepting who your mate is and giving yourself into their hands with complete trust to be good to you. Your mate is one fitted with authority, wisdom, knowledge, and understanding, to be **an help meet (suitable) for you**, to be good to you, and to care for you in all ways (mind, body, and spirit). Also, they are made to see that all is well with you, and to intercede with God on your behalf.

Surrender to God also, for He is your help and the head of your relationship. He is suitable and victorious in all things concerning you, and the Son intercedes with the Father on your behalf, always; Who did surrender Himself for you with great price. He knows **all** your relationships: mate to mate, parent to child, friend to friend, employer to employee, sibling to sibling, all relationships. Make Him your head and guide in all your relationships. You will be more at peace because He knows all hearts and can direct you on how to handle yourself in those relationships and circumstances. He knows what is good and knows when things are amiss before they play out, so He can save you from much heartache and errors.

Give yourself completely: let your heart, mind, and spirit be toward your mate. Be one with the person you are in commitment with. To be one with someone you must exhibit a heart, mind, and spirit of unity. There is no separation. This unit begins at you and ends at your mate; it is the same for them (it begins at them and ends at you), and you are one in God, meaning you are both wrapped in God.

This is the way God sees you, as a unit. While you are joined, you are both innocent or you are both guilty; you are partners; you are one. It takes much prayer and intercession that God may have mercy on one partner and use them to cover the other. To cover someone does not mean you ignore nor condone their mess, neither do you enable them. To cover them means you submit them to God to repair their breach as you bear them up with the strength God instilled in you. You are also responsible to hold each other accountable, that you may be presentable before God and man.

When you are obedient and submitted, you and your mate and

God are one in relationship. It is He that makes your relationship complete. When He is missing, there is trouble lurking (between mates, between parent and child, between friends, between employer and employee, between siblings, between all relationships).

When you resist your partner, you fight against yourself and also against God, Who is leading you in your relationship. If you attempt to destroy your partner, you are destroying yourself.

Lead a life of submission; it is required of you.

If you acknowledge that God, your Creator, is in Heaven, and that Christ, the Son of God, Who gave His life for you, is alive and in Heaven above, then submit to Him.

If you are a husband, submit to your mate; if you are a wife, submit to your mate. Your mate needs that love and care God promised them in you as an help meet for each other.

If you are a parent, submit to motherhood or to fatherhood. That child is depending on you, and God is watching to see how you treat the gifts He gave you. Be good to them always.

What ever your purpose, submit to it; don't lose your life without accomplishing the thing you were sent here to do. And, what about those who will be affected or suffer because you did not do your part? What ever your career, submit to it. There are assignments that must be done; there must be order. God is trusting you; be faithful in your journey. Again, lives may be touched and affected no matter how lowly your career or that job.

If you are in a best friendship with someone, submit to that great friendship. You were committed to that friend from the moment you gave and received that title of best friend. Be good to each other because it is a treasured thing.

If you are a pet owner, submit to it. God cares greatly about animals too. Be good to them because you were committed to them from the day you took them in, and they have no one but you. Love them and receive their love. Never place your animal above the life and well-being of the people in your family, but remember they are indeed family also and have great value in God's eyes.

Now then,...

When you are obedient and still you feel much pressure in your life, it is happening so God can effect change in you. Don't fight against the change in order to hold on to your old self; He sees that you need to be different, so lose yourself in Him. The way you feel, think, walk, talk, believe, and everything else, just let it go and embrace the change.

Coal (carbon) needs much pressure to become a diamond, and He's taking you from a piece of coal to a perfect diamond. Notice, I didn't say flawless, because some **flaws** add value and rarity to a diamond and are necessary for the purpose and use of that diamond.

Coal is a combustible mineral substance, and it is messy. It is capable of being very useful and helpful or powerful and destructive. Also, it is very easily crushed and very easily destroyed. When it passes through the fire it ignites and is very easily used up, and when it passes through the water it is made of non-effect.

As with the coal, so it is with you also. Are you filled with trouble, creating messy situations? Are you easily annoyed or angered? Do you stay seething for long periods of time, and is it hard to let things go? Do you instigate things to also make others angry or try to incite others to be as angry as you are? Are you excitable or high-strung? If the answer to all or any of these questions is yes, you are in a combustible state of being; you catch fire and explode by the slightest means but you are also filled with passion misdirected. As you are, you are useful and have power. You are capable of being very helpful or very destructive. You are very easily hurt, crushed, and bruised; you are very sensitive and easily destroyed. When you pass through difficult or stressful situations that ignite you, your strength gets used up and you have nothing left. Also, when bad situations are so many that they overflow you, it leaves you powerless, and no matter what you try it doesn't work.

Let God change you into a diamond. He applies strategic heat and pressure to you and your life; you will feel strength, and you may feel some growing pains as you begin to change, but in the end you will say, 'Thank You."

Moving onward,...

A diamond is a desired and treasured substance, but no one ever knows the true cost by which it came to be so exquisite.

A diamond is a pure or nearly pure form of carbon. The natural form of it is a clear cubic crystal, and is the hardest of all known minerals. It forms under conditions of extreme temperature and pressure. A diamond may be found in igneous rocks. It is transparent, flawless, or almost flawless, and when cut and polished it is valued as a gem. It is the most valuable of precious stones. Though mainly colorless, it is often tinted brown, red, orange, pink, yellow, green, blue, purple, black, etc., by impurities. Diamonds also have industrial uses, as in cutting and perforating other minerals.

You are a precious gem.

As God's diamond, you are made pure or nearly pure. You are free from darkness, your walls are made solid, and there is nothing hidden. You were made hard, unbreakable by most situations, and made to endure what would break or crush others. You are rendered adamant for His purposes. **Fear them not, neither be dismayed at their looks**. You were perfectly formed and molded as you experienced trials, tribulations, hardships, and stress to extreme measures. You were pressed then spewed out by life, where you sat waiting, until God unearthed and cleaned you up for purpose. You, being found in the igneous rock that is or was your life, are now exceptionally strong because you were tried by fire unto perfection. You no longer ignite by such means but now are unaffected, though everything around you may have burned to ashes.

God's chosen are transparent to all, so their beauty may be seen to their core. Still, there are some marked for greatness who endured things unspeakable which tainted them; or, maybe you were tainted by the environment in which you were raised. Healed, but forever tainted, with your forever testimony. Forever changed to whatever breathtaking color pleased God. This color that will have all people in awe of you and also treasure you as you express your testimony (the reason for your glorious color).

There is none quite like you. You contain too many facets (of your way: kind, caring, faithful, true, selfless, etc.), too much depth (of character), and you are so rich a color (of personality and experience). All these contained in you that you cannot be duplicated or simulated. Though tainted with the deepest and richest of color, still, you are not opaque (shut up). The Light still shines beautifully through you and draws many to that magnificent Light you reflect. You are the hardest and most valuable of precious stones. You are unshakable in your purpose, too hard to cut, break, or pierce by your adversaries; you stand in strength and victory. You are a sharp threshing instrument used by God to effect change in others.

To fight and resist surrendering became instinct to most because it is required for survival in this world, but to yield takes much strength, and courage, and trust. So, be strong and courageous, and trust with all your might, for to surrender to God, your relationships, and all that is good, is to submit to a better, greater, and victorious you.

VIII
Acknowledge

Admitting that you are aware of someone or something and showing appreciation is a key element in your love relationship with God and others. You must acknowledge them, their presence in your life, and their good toward you.

Does it not pierce you when someone you love ignores you and everything about you?

Does it not make you radiate when the person you love speaks well of you and shows you just how much your existence in their life is treasured?

It is no different with God or others.

It is a thing of great meaning, to express gratitude, or to have it expressed to you.

Do you see God daily in the things around you or in the things done on your behalf? If you do, then thank Him in sincerity. If you don't see Him, take a moment and feel His love for you, then look again.

Do you see the things your mate, family, children, friends, and others do for you daily, and do you hear their expressions of gratitude to you? If you do, reciprocate to them. If you do not, take a moment and look at them and their actions through eyes of love. Now, hear their words with an accepting heart. You will then see and hear them clearly in the way that they express themselves.

Meet them on their level of expression with sincerity. Don't judge them by the standards of your friend's husband or wife, nor by what another family member does or says. Don't judge them by their older or younger sibling, nor by another person's child. Don't judge them by what another friend does, nor by ideas that you dream anyone to be.

Appreciate who you have or who is before you, and sincerely accept their form of expression of goodness to you. If their form of expression to you is severely lacking, don't rail against them; they may be doing the best they know.

Some people simply don't know how to behave in relationships and would do better if they knew. Some simply lack confidence and may be fearing rejection, or may feel it makes them look weak to show such gratitude or to be that open. Don't withhold yourself from someone who is just ignorant of how to behave; be good to them. As time passes, and as your relationship grows in strength and trust, your form of expressions to them will teach and guide them.

Let your love and your good expressions teach them, not the words of your mouth in criticism. What if the way you expressed your gratitude to God caused you to hear His voice from Heaven saying, 'That's just not good enough. Why can't you do this or that?" Wouldn't it pierce your heart, knowing that you were sincere and doing the best you knew, but it was rejected? Just as God does, so should all people also receive all acknowledgment to them in the sincerity which it was given.

Gratitude comes in many forms. The easiest and simplest form is saying, 'Thank you." The greatest form is to name each thing. It also varies according to each person, because different people treasure different things and forms of expressions. In the middle, there is a very wide range of words and deeds, and at times no words at all, only a look, a touch, or a smile. For some mates the only form of expression they know to give is provision or that paycheck; acknowledge them with words and let your actions also show them appreciation. Over time they may learn to give words to you as well, if not, then continue to meet them at their level of expression with sincerity; know and accept them as they are. Words aren't the only way; any form of gratitude from a sincere heart will do; reciprocate to them.

When you breathe, do you recognize God and thank Him for putting that breath and life into you?

When things go ill with you and you feel like your breath would leave you, do you not cry out for His help?

So, why then when you are well, would you not recognize and appreciate that He holds your life and breath in His hand and allows you to breathe with every breath you take?

Do you see God in the elements He created or how He keeps and defends you daily?

Do you see the way your mate helps with the laundry and how your mate helps with the children?

Stroke your mate or loved one with love and gratitude for all they do. Do not strike your mate or loved one with wicked words and evil intentions; it pierces more than you know. Every strike may leave a scar that is unhealed beneath, which hurts to the touch because the wound goes that deep. A body (heart, mind, and spirit) covered in such scars will hurt even by an intended loving hug: this is called being misunderstood, so make your love clear. An intended loving touch hurts because now they are at a point where they expect no good thing, so your hug feels like a chokehold to them. Check your grip (ways and words), and make sure you are being gentle and nurturing; there are undertones and subtexts to all that is said and done, so be pure with your mate or loved one.

Never bring your mate, loved one, or anyone in your life to this wounded state because you and that relationship may never be able to return from it. Only God can then heal that wounded spirit, heart, and mind; He may then give them healed and whole to another who was made to appreciate them. If you receive anyone in such a wounded state, please, be good to them as God heals them. He gave them to your life in that state because He knows the nurturing care He equipped you to give to that one. Stroke your mate and others in sincerity and love.

In our love relationship with God, He does punish ungratefulness. This would be so unfortunate for us when it is so simple to say "Thank you."

In our love relationships with our mates and others, many of these relationships have failed and are damaged and crippled because of the lack of communication, appreciation, and gratitude.

Acknowledge yourself. You are important in this world and was created for a purpose and other assignments. You are not an accident, or mistake, or worthless, or useless; others may view you as such, but you are God's perfect creation. When God thought of this thing in the world that He needed or wanted to be done, He thought of whom would do this thing exactly as pleased Him, and He thought of you and only you. He then caused you to be conceived exactly how and exactly when and exactly by whom you were. He formed your body in the womb exactly as you were, and He equipped you to get that purpose done, and all else He desires.

As we grow, it becomes our duty and responsibility to seek and follow that purpose to which we were created. Ask Him. The earlier in life that we receive the knowledge of whom we are meant to be, the more potent and effective life we will live. When we not just believe but know this truth of whom we are and walk in it, the less confused we will be, the less mistakes we will make, and the less people we will hurt. It is a most precious thing to know exactly who you are, your duty in this world, and to see the lives that you affect by the good that you do as you walk in your purpose.

Know your own worth. Never assume nor decide your value from the words or treatment of others who don't know the true you. Know who you are from the thoughts of God however He speaks to you, and through the deep passion, desire, and drive He gave you. Acknowledge it is true. Don't just believe but come to know it; be confident in it and in yourself that God indeed made you able to accomplish it.

When you know what you were born to do, seek God for instruction. Ask Him for help and He will guide you. He did not send you without clearing a path for you, and when necessary He will carve a new path in order that you will succeed. He will give you wisdom, knowledge, and understanding of exactly how to accomplish it. However He speaks to you, He will let you know what is good and what is not, which deal to make and which deal to walk away from, who is good to have close to you and who is not.

Every thing is laid out for you; the delays, and detours, and the problems to your life come in lack of hearing and obedience. You may not hear properly, or may not understand what you hear. Maybe, you didn't wait for full counsel and full understanding, so you were not fully prepared to go forward. This is when errors occur, because you made a wrong step, or turned out of your prepared path. You may not like every thing you need to do to accomplish your purpose. If you don't follow instruction, or you skip a step in the plan, or you try to go your own way, all this is never good. Doing these wrong things, if you don't end up in a bad place or destroyed, you certainly won't get the full blessing you were supposed to receive, because you disobeyed and God didn't get the glory.

When He opens a way, there is no denying Him. In some things you have to move very quickly, and things go so rapid that it makes your head spin. You can't even think in that moment, but at the end you are standing in a great blessing that makes you marvel and thank Him. And, some things go very slowly, so slow you may have a creeping wonder and possible doubt, but you must trust and thank Him in your waiting and in your single step at a time moments.

The path you travel is vital. If one of your assignments in your purpose is to work as a janitor, still, walk in your path; it is a great service in the world. There are other janitors about, and they must walk in their path also. The task looks the same, and the description is the same, but the path created for you will touch the lives that only you were created to affect, and that means something. Have you ever seen or heard of that one standout genuine person on the job? They most likely are walking in their path. There is a person or persons like this in every field of work on earth, and it makes others take notice and celebrate them because they are real and faithful in everything. If this is not you, seek God and follow your path and it will be you being celebrated: not because you seek to be noticed, but because you are faithful.

Everyone was born to a purpose, and every purpose is different. Some were born to a lowly purpose, but all purposes are important. Some were brought into the world to nurture and affect one single life, and that single life was made to flourish and then nurture and affect ten lives or ten thousand lives, and so on. These are the beautiful ways of God. If your purpose seems small, don't despise it, perform it with love and all sincerity; it is great in God's eyes. If your purpose seems great, don't let pride swallow you up, perform it with love and all sincerity and be humble; this is pleasing before God and man. If you allow pride to swallow you up, God will remove you from your purpose or withhold it. If so, think of the many people now affected, or even that one special person now being without nurturing and who did not flourish. Also, that good never being done, that you and only you were responsible for accomplishing but failed to do. Acknowledge your purpose and your responsibility to accomplish it. To accomplish your purpose brings the help to the world and humanity that it yearns for and brings God the glory that belongs to Him.

IX
Hope

*H*ope is deep inner determination toward a thing. A fixed belief and expectation in a thing that is not yet tangible. What is your hope? Never stop believing. When all hope seems lost, desperation attacks and seeks to destroy. If God said it or gave you an image of it or gave you the passion for it, that was His promise to you, and so it shall be if you don't let go. You may have nothing now and you yearn for that better life, or you may feel neglected and forgotten, but Someone vital looks down and sees you and is acting on your behalf.

In all things there is order and time; some things are immediate and others take time, even years, but never let go. Make sure your hope is true so you don't spend wasted time hoping in a false thing that is not of God and is no good for you.

Whether male or female, are you with an emotional or physical abuser with no intervention or attempt to change?

Does that one keep abusing you while they say they are in the process of changing or trying to change?

Are they repentantly sorry (or seem so) each time they have abused you yet continue to have slip-ups or regress back to abuse after very small moments of better behavior?

If all or any answer is yes, now is not the time to hope in them or that relationship; this is a false hope; this is more than just you alone can help them through. Be no more their object of release. Walk away in wisdom when there is the first safe opportunity to do so. Then, forgive them and pray for them that they will receive healing, and move forward with your life as God heals you. God did not make you to be abused; He made you to be loved, honored, and cherished; hope in that, and reject anything and anyone that is against that.

Are you with a person that keeps using you, who always leaves you feeling less than who you are?

Do you have moments of clarity when you see and feel the actual disrespect that they truly hold for you?

Are you longing for a person who shows you no regard?

Do they show you repeatedly that they don't care one bit?

Do they show you always that their world is fine without you in it?

If you are in this experience, first ask yourself if God gave that person to your life and if that person is capable of treasuring you. Asking yourself these questions will have the obvious answer that will set you and half the public free. For the other half that is unsure, and maybe you still, ask yourself how they treat the people they say they love.

Are they faithful and true to others?

Are they kind, caring, and respectful?

These are all things that true love contain, and an individual capable of giving such love to you will genuinely exhibit these behaviors at some time in their life. When God gives love to you it is always true, and the person He intends to join you with will always be caused to exhibit these things in your presence at some time that you may see their beauty. If you have not experienced neither witnessed these things in the person you pine for, re-evaluate yourself and know what is true and who is true. Evaluating yourself will give you the answer that will set you and another quarter of the public free.

So, now we would have three-quarters of the public that is free from their false hope and self-abuse. For to stay in such relationships, whether one-sided or mutual, is self-abuse because you know that God gave you a better hope and intends better for you, yet your insecurities make you stay.

Now there is a remnant left. Some must go their way and learn to love themselves first, and some were made for God's glory who must hold on and maintain their hope. Of this remnant, if you are bound by marriage and they begin to try, hope in them and help them. If you are not bound by marriage, separate yourself and hope in them (at a distance) that they will hear and obey God to be good to you, and live while you wait.

Maybe you desire a path for your life that keeps being just beyond your fingertips. If so, seek God to know if that path is your true purpose on this Earth, it could make the difference between wasted years and a life full of passion and meaning.

When I look at my own purpose, or the purpose of others I know or know of, I have found that true purpose is usually connected with helping others or to the benefit of another besides one's self. It is never about making money nor the prospering and posturing of yourself. No matter what field of work, it is almost always about a heart of service and about filling a need. Also, the really awesome and very cool thing about Him is the connection and passion you will find inside yourself for the purpose He chose for you. It is the thing you feel driven to do even if you never made a penny.

You will also find that He knows you better than you think and even better than you know yourself because His choice will be something that suits you. When you consider or reflect on His choices, it will be something so natural to whom you truly are and something He will bring you out of your comfort zone to achieve. This comfort zone is only a hiding place, where many hide from their greatness or from greater accomplishments. When you connect with your purpose (this inner longing), **this** is true, hope in this; take strategic steps as He leads you and watch it come to pass.

If you have found your true purpose and still you have struggled, even for many years, and have not succeeded, it may be a case of **right thing but wrong way and wrong intentions**. Seek God for the right way. Or, just maybe you are not yet ready to handle where He wants to take you and you need a season of preparation and of waiting. Forcing the wrong thing or wrong way or having the wrong attitude and intentions will only cause harm; it will wreck you eventually and wreck those you intended to help. Believe, and take the steps He opens to you; also, submit as He changes and refines you. When you get there, never forget your journey and Who brought you through it all, and keep hoping in Him for the greatest level He desires you to reach.

Perhaps you are hoping for a better life in general. If you feel like you are just existing and believe there has to be something more, you are right, there is. If nothing is right, give it to Him and He will lead, teach, and guide you into His joy for you. Now, to those with what seems perfect: Your money is right, and your relationship is right, and your career is right. Also, your friends and your family are all good as can be. Everyone and everything around you is OK, but **you, you** are missing something. You will find what you are missing when you connect with God. Believe in Him, and believe in yourself that you are desperately loved by Him, and that you are or will be all He made you to be in all aspects of your life.

One must hope in himself always or will find himself fading away into obscurity. So, you must hope in God always because He keeps you connected to exactly who you truly are, and you will never become lost to yourself. Lost, such as when a wife and a mother hopes in her husband and her children, then her hope is realized in them because now they are exactly what she believed and longed for. He is great, and the children are grown and become great, then she is left lost and empty because she forgot to hope in herself also.

Never allow yourself to disappear into anyone else but God. He always sees you, even at times when others don't, and even when you may not see yourself clearly. He knows exactly who you are and will remind you and guide you, so you will always exude an air of confidence about you and others will never fail to be attracted to that. Even you will like yourself very much: not in an arrogant way but in self-appreciation and love.

Don't hope in false things that God didn't give you and has nothing to do with. The things that God said and did lead you to, hold on and believe in that with all your heart and He will bring it to pass in His good time.

Prayerfully you are now aware of what things in your life are true and what things are false and how to discern the difference, because God would not have you ignorant of the truth. Whatever you are believing God for, if it be true, hold on because He is able and He is faithful to do it. Just know that He will not forget nor forsake you, so do not let go. Always remember, if you do let go and lose hope you will also lose yourself because hope is vital to your thriving. With this knowledge now in you, if you see anyone in your journey that is lost or headed for that pit of hopelessness, allow God to use you as that needed instrument of help. You can be that help, even if only to pray or to connect them with one who will help more than you can.

Now, there is the eternal hope of God: hope in Him. Christ Jesus paid a ransom for you; through Him and by Him **all** things are possible, including the most precious gift of salvation, and that above all else you must believe. He is your greatest hope. Never let go. Be blessed and hope in God.

X
Trust & Faith

Trust: it is discerning, it learns and grows in strength, it is watered by kindness and good, and it is powered by faith (**complete** trust).

Faith is absolute and complete trust without any present tangible thing attached. You have faith in God, whom you have not seen. You have faith in your future, which you desire. You have faith in yourself: who you want to become. You believe beyond reason that your children will be all they were born to be, etc. Faith is the truth you stand in though you can't prove it. It is your unshakable belief that you live by and live for. Each individual has to possess his own faith: it is vital to life and a prospering spirit.

Faith pertaining to God: You must have faith in God in order to invite Him into your heart and life. You must believe that He exists and loves you. Believing His promises to you will come to pass is essential to your existence and prosperity. You must trust that His will for you is always what is best for you and the purpose He sent you to.

Many times in life, situations and circumstances place you at a crossroads within, where you fear and wonder many things not convenient. You wonder which way to go, you wonder if God's got you, and you wonder if you are in error. You wonder if God will ever deliver you, and you wonder what you can do to dig yourself out, whether God approves or not. Also, some wonder if there is even a God. But, in all your wondering, the emptiness you feel always matches your disbelief, accordingly, when your disbelief grows, so does the emptiness you feel inside. You must believe. You must trust. You must have faith.

When you trust Him, He sees and feels it, and the strength of your trust and faith causes Him to treasure you. When He treasures you, then, you will enter a period of refinement chosen by Him. In your refinement period, you may wonder if He truly loves you or if there is some great evil you have done for which you are being punished. This is so because He will allow things into your life and expose your life to hardships that make you feel the evil against you, which at times give you a feeling of helplessness. Yet, He is always present in your life and shields your mind and spirit, though your heart and body suffers. During this trying time, He brings you to know Him better and He brings you to know yourself better. He brings you to know your core-self. He brings you to full trust in Him, and He brings you to know that He is enough.

After your period of refinement is over, He will bless you beyond your imagination because you were faithful to Him and because He desires the best for you. In reflecting, you will realize His power in your life. Because of all you endured and because He showed you Himself, your trust and faith is now refined. Now you are past belief, and are past faith concerning Him: now you **know**. Now you know He exists. Now you know He is always present in your life. Now you know He is for your good. Now you know His word to you lives. Now you know you are His beloved. Now you know His word is true. Now you know there is no other God. Now you know yourself and see your purpose clearly. Now you know He is faithful and true. Now you know He loves you, and now you know how much He loves you. Now you are sensitive to your slipping feet and ways and can call Him, knowing He will catch you from falling. If you stumble or fall, now you know He will pick you up, dust you off, and set you back on the right path. Now you are sensitive to His direction. Now wisdom, knowledge, and understanding are firm within you. Now you live knowing.

What is it to live knowing? The answer is complicated to those without knowledge and simple to those who contain it. One hundred percent trust or full trust is faith, so what is one hundred percent faith or full faith? It is a level only few attain and a level only God can take you to through refinement: to get there costs much; there is indeed a great price but not monetary. To get to knowing, you must drink of His cup and carry the burden laid upon you. The greater the calling on your life, the greater the burden will be, and the more you will be made to drink from His cup. What is in His cup? Truth, unfiltered truth, and ability to endure what that truth brings to you. After suffering that cost of whatever He sees fit for you and whatever your calling demands, if you remain faithful, He will take you past faith into knowing. You now see Him, you now know Him, you now know truth: it is fixed in you, and you now understand things concerning Him. He gives you precious sight and precious knowledge; you now live on a different plain with Him, where nothing can easily separate you from Him.

How difficult is it to deceive someone who holds the truth, one who holds truth about their Maker, and truth about themselves?

Those who hold the truth are not so easily deceived. It is no longer just about you believing what you cannot see because you do see Him, and you do hear Him. All concerning Him is now certain in you and is now fact because He now has shown you Himself and has now proven Himself to you. He has placed the evidence of Himself in you and has fixed it there: you are sealed unto Him. And, can anyone or anything easily rob you of a fixed knowledge? No. You now know He is real and that His power is real. You live it, you breathe it, and you walk in it. It is a permanent knowledge of Him and His power and His presence in your life.

So, you have excelled in trust over to faith, does this mean that trust is no longer in you? No; it simply means trust is fixed in you. Then, you have excelled in faith over to knowing, does this mean that faith is no longer in you? No; it means that faith is also now fixed in you along with trust. Now you are in knowledge, the knowledge of God, and this is now fixed in you. The knowledge of God is great and deep and wide: never cease to excel in the knowledge of Him, forevermore. Trust and faith never left you and will never leave you; they are never irrelevant nor useless in your higher level because they are a part of the foundation of your knowledge. Whenever you get weak, He will allow them to remind you of just who He is and of just who you are. They will always strengthen and encourage you, and will take you higher in knowledge, as high and deep and wide in Him as He desires to take you.

Faith in your future, in yourself, in your children, and in all you desire is aided by the faith you have in God. The more you believe in Him, the more you will believe good things for yourself and for those around you. When you live knowing, you also know that His plans for you and those around you are real, true, and will come to pass. You know that His hand is to the good of you and your household because

He has shown Himself true in your life. You believe His promises concerning you and your household because you have seen His word unfold and come to fruition before your eyes. You know that just as promise numbers one through five have come to pass as He said, so will promise numbers six through twenty in His perfect time. You know, because you have seen Him tend to the needs of you and your loved ones. You know, because your loved ones are a living proof, and you stand a living witness to yourself and to the world. You have the advantage over your enemies, not only with truth and knowledge but also now with experience, and your experience is not just a reference point but is also where your power lies.

Is there not something familiar in this new situation and crossroads?

Do you not feel the déjà vu feeling?

You know the way of victory: trust speaks, faith speaks, experience speaks, and the knowledge of God speaks....

Trust says, **hold on**. Faith says, **He will do it again for you**. Experience says, **you didn't break before and you won't break now**. The knowledge of God says, **walk this way**. The promise of God says, **I will deliver you**. The word of God says, **you are Mine**. Your witness says, **with God all things are possible**. Your Maker says, **I am God and there is none besides Me, therefore believe in Me**. And, your testimony says, **bless the Lord, oh my soul, and all that is within me, bless His Holy name**, and **thank You**.

XI
Love

What is love? Love is a gift of deep and abiding connection and commitment given from God. It is the sharing and giving of your complete self to the heart and spirit of another; no part of you is held back and no part of you is hidden. Wanting and seeking the other person's best interest and that of the relationship before your own is a fact of true love. Another fact of love is desiring no harm to the one you love or to yourself. Also, seeking after no thing that will harm, injure, or dissolve the love relationship and harboring no ill will. Acceptance of the whole person and faithfulness in spirit: This is true love tended to.

A faithful spirit will keep you through to the other side of a dark time when your heart and mind won't. Sometimes a desire to run away (physically or emotionally) may come, but you stay and you work through the issues that made you feel that way. Your love relationship with God is training ground for your love relationship with your mate and family, never forget that. In like manner, as you love and care for your relationship with God, you are also to love and care for others.

There is one broad manner of love given from God to every heart; though some choose not to embrace it and let it fill them, still, it is given. When you embrace it and let it fill you, then, you will find that this love is unconditional. In us, as humans, there are also different levels of intimacy and different levels of desires and willingness to this love. Among humans we should carry or hold the highest level of intimacy with our mates: not speaking sexually but speaking on an emotional level. We should also carry or hold the highest level of willingness and desire toward our mate.

As in your relationship with God, there should be no measure of selfishness involved with your mate. In relationships, it is easier for some to give their life to save their mate or loved one than to give their life to save a stranger, it is not impossible, only much easier for most people to do. This is a grand form of selflessness. There are many less-grand selfless acts that love does daily, and though many may go unnoticed or unacknowledged or neglected, never allow that to change what love does.

    As you love God, so must you love your mate and others. See your mate and others through God's love which He placed in you. You will find that you are able to show them that unchanged and unconditional love, even through their faults and their errors. You will find that you show love when others wouldn't expect it. You will also find that it discerns and enables you to give it when and how it is most needed.

    Love that is pure will never intentionally harm, neither does it intentionally enable bad behaviors. If love discerns that tough love is needed, then that is what should be given; this is the kind of love God gives at needed times. It may seem cruel to the recipient or some onlookers, but is a necessary love that is made for correction of the recipients errors, and is never and should never be given with selfish or wicked intentions.

    Love lasts through time and distance. Love accepts and adapts. Love compromises for the good health of the relationship and is unconditional. It sees, hears, feels, and discerns. Love sees a hidden hurt or brokenness. It hears the things one cannot find words for. It feels the pain that another cannot express. It discerns and understands beyond the natural.

    Never give love with the intent or expectation of receiving it or anything else in return. If you express your love seeking anything in return you will no doubt be left severely wounded and unsatisfied. There will be no one to blame but your own expectations (things you require as appropriate or rightfully due) that shouldn't have been. Jesus loves us, not so we can love Him back or for Him to receive anything from us, He only loves us so purely because He feels it. He wants our love and the things and praises we give but does not expect it, that's why He gave us free will, so we would choose Him, not because we felt obligated but because we desired Him. In this same manner, you should express the love, kindness, and care you feel to others; but, do not expect or feel you have a right to reciprocation in any manner.

Whether with an acquaintance, co-worker, friend, or in a relationship, maybe you have done so or have experienced the offense of someone doing something, seemingly, out of the love and kindness of their heart. Then, you or that someone forces obligation on the other, or expects a like kindness or act of love to be returned, who then complains when the expectations aren't met. This is an act of selfishness and should never be done in such manner. You cannot offer up or force someone's heart or pocket to take turns or meet your desire; it is manipulative, inconsiderate, disrespectful, and selfish.

If you are in a mutually committed friendship, relationship, or marriage, then there indeed are some required duties to and from your mate or loved one, such as, being good to each other, and sharing your complete self. Likewise, they ought to do the same because that is the level of intimacy God created for such relationships. Your relationship with God is the same. If you call yourself His, and He cares for you, then surely He expects certain actions and certain respects from you. He is expectant of you because you called yourself His, or you received His love and said you loved Him too, which is a commitment to Him. A commitment is a binding promise. Outside of that, He only hopes in mankind to make right and just choices and that they will feel the love He gives. If you feel it, receive it.

When you receive someone's love, be it God or your mate or your child or your best friend, and also give them your love in return, you are indeed obligated to love. You must then behave accordingly and also reciprocate; if you do not, then you lie, or you never truly knew what love **is**. How are you committed to someone and continue selfishly to do as you please, without regard to them, acknowledgment of them, or showing love to them? If you are not giving such connection with your mate or loved one, then let God's love heal you, and teach you how to share yourself, and guide you to be good to that mate or loved one. If you are not receiving such connection with your mate or loved one, then show them how love behaves, and let that love heal them, teaching them how to share themselves. Then, that pure love now in them will guide them to be good to you.

The saying goes, **love hurts**, and many songs echo the same, but it is not so. Love is pure, and true, and contains no faults. As *humans* (*post-sin*), it is our inabilities, selfishness, insecurities, and lack of understanding, which causes us to be bruised, wounded, and hurt; it also causes us to bruise, wound, and hurt others. Yes, it is because of the strength of love within us why we are so sensitive to feel these pains so greatly. But, it is not love itself that causes the pains, it is the **corrupters** of love that grieve hearts. The causes of pain include: our expectations, meanness, selfishness, pride, fear, distrust, spitefulness, jealousy, and all other corrupted things that keeps love from being given and received in its pure and sincere form.

The greatest of all **corrupters** is expectation: our own expectations within us. Our expectations are sometimes unfounded, or not real and true, so they do fail. Again, sometimes they are real and true and we deserve what we expect, but we have no control over other people, and rightly so. Nevertheless, when expectations fail they are responsible for some of the deepest and gravest wounds and pains mankind has ever felt to the core of their being, and has also sadly taken certain lives.

Now, jealousy is linked with love worldwide with sayings such as, **he or she is so jealous because they really love me**, or **he or she really loves me because they are so jealous**; this is wrong. Jealousy is a form of rage because a situation is not the way one desires it to be. Love does not and should not have any connection to rage. This jealousy, whether the cause was unfounded or just, is rage on the inside; when it is harbored, it increases and festers. In jealousy, unfounded thoughts and fears usually arise; then, being the uncontrollable thing it is, it begins to spill out onto its target and anyone who gets in the way. It may begin as cruel words and accusations, and such things as we are all guilty of, but as it continues to fester and become toxic, then, irrational thoughts, or thoughts of violence, or acts of violence may erupt.

Rage breeds many things with it; let it all go by open communication, and gain true understanding of the situation. Also, remember that the only one you can control is yourself. Rage and wrath belong to God and are emotions we cannot handle. In jealousy, one has laid love down and picked up rage, wrath, fears, resentfulness, and wicked imaginations in its place. They are equipped to destroy the very one and thing they professed to love, and/or the one they blame for the feelings they now carry.

In this world, haven't those emotions been reserved for an enemy?

Surely you wouldn't invite nor welcome-in these emotions concerning someone you love?

Is your love (loved one) your enemy?

Is your love (loved one) your adversary?

Love is not jealous. Love understands, seeks truth, and does not seek to control. Love gives light in your relationship. Feelings of rejection and neglect breeds and feeds jealousy, which is an issue within. No matter what a person does, know that you are valuable and that the loss is theirs. Many times in relationships, issues cause hurt, pain, and anger, but one should always keep rage and wrath out and never embrace them.

Many say to their love, "You're my heart." If it were naturally so, would you be violent and cruel to your own heart if it were in your hands? Would you not tend to it at all times, making sure that it was well?

Women, give pure love to your loved ones, especially to the mate whose love you received and gave your love to in return. You are obligated to that love, to be true and good to them always, and to never be deliberate against them nor wicked and violent in any form.

Men, give pure love to your loved ones, especially to the mate whose love you received and gave your love to in return. You are obligated to that love, to be true and good to them always, and to never be deliberate against them nor wicked and violent in any form.

All people, give pure love to God, your Creator, whose love you received and gave your love to in return. You are obligated to that love, to be true, good, and faithful to Him always, and to never be deliberate against Him nor wicked and violent in any form.

No human is free from errors, but never be wicked nor deliberately so against God, nor against mankind. Let love heal as it should, and let love light your way.

XII
Truth

Truth gives light and enlightenment.
God is love. God is truth. Where God is, there is light by wisdom, knowledge, and understanding. Truth frees hearts, souls, and minds. Truth is information that is pure and free from all evil intentions. It is what God gives to all who are willing and ready to hear. The same is how it should be given by us to each other so that it will be received well.

Some tell information in order to punish and wound another; this is truth, tainted. Some give information spitefully, sarcastically, etc. Give truth pure and plain, without wickedness. It is not a weapon to smite those you should care for, it is a kind gift of knowledge. Many prefer and choose lies and falsehood because it satisfies some temporary need in them, but eventually, the soul of that person will cry out for truth. Truth is not always liked or desired, but knowledge is good, and it causes growth and clearer understanding, when given in an acceptable manner. The knowledge of some truths may unintentionally bring pain to the heart of the one receiving it, but the manner and timing in which it was given will aid in the healing process, because it was truth given with love.

Within truth is a fact most would like destroyed and forgotten, and it must needs be spoken on at this time, for it is desired that the hatred cease. For those with a **different** love, desire, and attraction, from this day onward, let Truth and Knowledge be firm in you, know that homosexuality is not sin. It is not evil, nor is it vile before Him. You are greatly loved and accepted of the Lord. He made you, and all made by Him is good. You possess a given love that is true, good, and worthy to be given and received.

Before God there is no straight love, with the assumption that same sex love is bent or crooked and needs to be fixed. There is only, as perceived by man, a **different** love. God made you to love **differently**, and it is a good and pure love. It is the same true and unconditional love that He gives to all mankind for their mates. However, in your love (again, as perceived by man), God has wrapped up and given you a **different** desire, attraction, and form or type of intimacy with your chosen mate. So, this makes it a **different** love in their eyes. For most, it is unacceptable, but it is, indeed, a blessed and given love.

Do not hate nor slay yourselves, and do not be ashamed, God is on your side and is fighting for you, that you will be accepted in this world. It is not happenstance that the heart of your present leader was changed toward you. However the process took place, and whatever ignited his heart to turn, it was indeed God that brought the change and gave him the courage to admit it publicly. Surely, that task was not an easy thing, neither was it the popular thing for a leader to do, for there are many stone-throwers in such cases. Know, that God Himself is fighting for you, so don't give up on yourself or on Him. The love God places in your heart is pure and good, so, embrace it, with your whole being. God is not fixed on gender: He sees heart, mind, and spirit. He chooses and connects spirit beings together, and it doesn't matter what gender that spirit being is wrapped in.

Every work of God is good, who is man to say, 'What corrupt thing is this?" That, surely is sin, to cast off and reject the work of God's own hand. When truth, wisdom, knowledge, and understanding comes, light is given, and who can reject it? Besides, if you turn your back, it doesn't change, it remains.

There is a great lie erected in order to slay a people that God loves, and they are hated without a cause; He finds no fault in the love their heart feels because He placed that love there. However, people of all religions, even those that serve other gods, and even some who deny God's existence, seek to strike them down, hoping they will perish. But, I say to you, they are God's children, and are counted righteous unto Him, when they embrace Him. They are blessed unto Him: He will defend them and punish those who seek to destroy them. Cease the hatred, abuse, and slaying of God's people, or judgment will come swiftly to you. Who will you then run to, and where will you turn, from the face of God?

If you love **differently** (as men say), and are homosexual, gay, lesbian, bisexual, or transgender (with whomever you love), do not despair, God sees you and all your thoughts and feelings, and you are not in sin. You are His, and He gave you that heart, and that love, and that body, and that mate you trusted Him for, so be not ashamed, and do not slay yourself because of what your heart feels.

Homosexuality is a given form/way/expression of love, and He will choose your mate (a mate fit for you), if you trust Him to. He is speaking to you now, know that He is your God and will defend you. Feel Him now reaching out His hand to you, take it; embrace His love and choose Him. Trust Him to fight for you; hope in Him. He is not against you, He seeks to defend you. Not all understood Christ, not all understand God (though they profess to), and not all will understand you; even those that love **differently**, as you do, may not understand you. He has made each person with many different facets to them; each has a specific purpose they were born to accomplish, and has a unique life they were created to live. So, do not fight amongst yourselves, only accept and love each other.

To all mankind: know, that some are made in the womb, some are made as children, and some are made as adults. God is able and does create (make) in the heart of humans, the love, desires, and preferences that He sees best for them, and will guide them in the direction that will allow their life and purpose to be fulfilled. Beloved, do not tear at each other, nor struggle against the beliefs of those without knowledge. There is not just one absolute to whom you are, or when you were made, nevertheless, you were indeed **made** so by the God of Heaven. All are flowers in God's garden, even so, flowers blossom and bloom at a time unique to them, and according to their care and nurture.

Do the flowers in a garden (acting like weeds) seek to destroy the other that bloomed in May instead of April?

What of the flowers that bloom in winter, are they despised and scorned?

Is it not a true flower because it bloomed later than others?

Did not the same Gardener plant them all, and, does He not find them all lovely to behold?

Love and support one another; you are all beautiful. You are not vile but beautiful before Him. He has never destroyed any for their love. He destroyed only those of **all** persuasions who were disobedient, and they who caused harm to those that love Him, and as such, Sodom was fallen. Not for homosexuality was Sodom destroyed, but for wickedness, rapes, and grave abuse against one another and those that love God. The offenders desired even to rape the two Angels of the Lord.

Read all of God's word for yourself, and let Him open your understanding. Do not accept the twisted interpretations passed on for centuries in order to slay you. Do not hate nor turn from God because of something misrepresented that He did not intend nor desire you to suffer.

Are there not vile, wicked, LGBT that deserve to be punished at God's hand? And so, they are punished.

Are there not vile and wicked humans among you? This is what God sees and punishes.

If God punished an area that was predominantly one race, religion, or like set of peoples for their wickedness, would it make that entire race, or that entire religion, or that entire set of peoples an abomination? No.

The unfaithfulness and wickedness being done is the abomination, not the love God places in a man, or the race, or the religion, or the set of peoples. After God's punishment for wickedness, should that give any in that group, race, religion, or people good cause to be perpetually offended, and to despise the name of God and His existence? No.

Open your heart and see where the error of your people lay and know truth; know that you are not vile because someone's actual sins were punished, and do not internalize the reproach of men without knowledge.

Sodom and Gomorrah has been cited much against homosexuals, but God will reveal Himself with love to His people. The truth concerning Sodom is, both of Lot's daughters were married. When the angels came to the house, their husbands were out with the homosexuals like themselves, among the gang of the cheering town's people. These people, which were most of the town, were pillaging, robbing, beating, raping, attacking, and doing other heinous crimes against one another and against the **very** few that resisted them. Nevertheless, God desired to save all who Lot loved in the city and Lot's entire household, which included them, **these homosexuals**. Had they chosen to leave the city with Lot and their wives, they would have been saved, but they refused to leave the brutal gang and the rest of town's people that cheered them on. They refused to return home even in the dawn of day, so they perished with their cohorts.

Lot lingered, I believe in hopes they would change their minds and come home, but they did not, and Lot almost perished in waiting. These husbands left their wives unloved and unwanted. They left them filled with feelings of neglect and low self-esteem, thinking there was no man on earth left for them. They thought no men were left that they deserved or that would want them. The older convinced the younger of these vile things, but had the younger not felt worthless within she would not have submitted to the words and plans of her sister. Surely they knew it was only those towns and not the world that was being destroyed. Surely they knew their uncles and cousins were well and that other men existed in the world. They had to know that other men existed that were not yet wed. Yet, they spoke with such self-hatred against themselves, causing them to bring a curse upon themselves by each one raping their father. Still, these husbands would have been saved by the merciful God.

God even desired to save the entire city, including all the homosexuals, including the gang or gangs, and including all the guilty town's people that encouraged the crimes, but no heart was worthy. The wickedness and crimes within the city was so great it reached God in Heaven and affected Him. There could not be found ten that were not guilty of crimes or encouraging crimes, so He made the wicked to cease. Think of the fingers of the hands and imagine, doing right or desiring to do right could not be found in that very small amount from a whole entire city. All were guilty of committing or encouraging severe crimes against one another and whoever dared to enter that city.

Sodom was a city overrun by crime and violence, especially at night, so, the Angels sought to wait in the streets to witness it for themselves. Think of any innocent person of whatever persuasion or orientation having to endure life in that city, and having no one to turn to for help, with **all** the town's people cheering on the wicked. If the ten the Lord spoke of included Lot's household, which contained six people as written, then there would only be a need for four additional people. But, whether four more or ten, they could not be found anywhere in that city.

Though the two husbands were guilty of crimes, not for whom they were but for the wickedness they did, still, they would have been saved because of God's love for Abraham and Lot. But, they were not able to see God's hand of love, by way of Lot, extended to them and did not believe. Though many homosexuals dwelled within, had the town's people not been so cruel, there would be no destruction to speak of. Just as when God sent the flood and destroyed all but Noah and his family, it was for the cause of wickedness, not for anyone's sexuality which God made.

Throughout the Bible, you will see the times when God destroyed people and lands, such was for a cause of wickedness and disobedience, not for a race or religion or orientation. He has the power to destroy, but there is no error in Him, so He never would destroy anyone for such causes if they are not against Him or those that love Him. In the case of religion, He allows people free will to choose who they will serve. He only destroyed those who did grave things and were unfaithful while professing to love Him. Therefore, patiently giving the rest that did not call themselves His people the opportunity to choose Him. Read, and know God for yourselves. He desires you to truly know Him, and He desires your love.

There are things that displease God with **all** orientations concerning love and relationships. These things include promiscuity, using others, giving yourselves away to be used, abuse (mental and physical), coercion, rape, trickery, lies, deceit, cunningness, brutality, adultery, and all other wickedness and forms of wickedness. Also, do not be like the daughters of Lot. Know that you are worthy of love and care. Know that you are worthy of being desired and will be by the one made for you. You are not worthless. Do not settle because you feel insecure. Do not hide from good love because someone did not love themselves and mistreated or abused you. Do not hate yourself because someone did not know the treasure you are and did not know how to treat you. Do not lose hope in true love with another because someone used you to hide from whom they truly were. Do not succumb to bitterness or despair from any neglect you experienced. Do not embrace anyone's vile view of you, only embrace the loving view God has of you.

There is a multitude of truth concerning all life and the ways of God and man. A small portion has been given to you, so that those affected may live in peace and be comforted.

To all mankind: Open yourselves and be humble that you may receive of God and be enlightened to all truth concerning all things in this life you live; He desires this for you.

Love God, love one another purely, and live in truth, this pleases God.

Postface

This book, all chapters, every page, every word, and cover to cover is, indeed, a perfect Word for a people in need, so they may live in truth with Wisdom, Knowledge, and Understanding. Every chapter is truth revealed: truth of righteousness, truth of sin, truth of confusion, truth of praise, etc. It is enlightenment from cover to cover, so all may live in a better way.

It is good for all to come to Knowledge, to walk in Wisdom and Understanding, and to know of the grace and love that abides and is offered for them to receive. It is just, for all rejected and despised to know the peace bestowed upon them, so they will walk in power.

It is expedient and expeditious for mankind to learn what is acceptable and just in His sight; don't think to know Him with false assumptions, but truly come to know Him. Will you fight against God because you think to know, or will you listen and hear Him? Your own thoughts may lead you astray; render your heart, mind, and spirit unto God. Let Him fill you with wisdom, knowledge, and understanding about Himself, about you, about purpose, and about how to live this life effectively.

How is this done? How do you render yourself to Him? Believe in Him, then let your heart, mind, and spirit be willing toward Him; He will take it from there. As one would open themselves up in relationship with a mate they truly desire, in like manner or even greater, we do open ourselves up in our relationship with Him, or should be willing to do so, and He will do the rest.

~

The premise (basis, nexus, foundation, root, core) of this book came out of a need, which was answered well by God Himself. The need was to understand God better, to be clear in hearing when He speaks, and to know that indeed God Himself was speaking. There were deeper lessons that needed to be learned, and deeper truths to be understood. Learning to trust Him completely was necessary. Then, following Him that long mile while being attentive and obedient the whole way. Also, letting uncertainties, preconceived notions, and wrong judgments fall by the way, and accepting all of His heart and will. That journey and this book took seven difficult years to complete and an additional one and half years of processing and refinement. You have read well, now be blessed.

~

Lord, thank You for trusting me. Sustain me, O God, for I am obedient; Thy servant heareth.
God be glorified.

Encouragement

What or who is your adversary?
Are you in your own way?
Are you impeding what God is desiring to do?
Are others against you without a cause?

Hold on to God. You will make it through, and you will not be swallowed up. You are still saved. God is with you, and He never left your side. Any reproach you endure because of your suffering and because of your obedience to God will be rewarded with good by He Who is Holy because of your submission in faithfulness to Him.

Stay on your true path. The thing that may seem wrong is indeed of God and is good for you to walk through because you are inside obedience to God. The path He is leading you through is untrodden, and the road may be very long, but be assured He is in full control and victory is with Him; turn neither to the left nor the right from Him. Your adversary is whoever or whatever impedes your Godly designed purpose from being carried out as God desires. It is never for you to deal with an adversary. Your only duty and care is, not to go after your adversary, but to walk on your designed path, and do only the things that are in and attached to your purpose.

An adversary (natural or spiritual) of you and your purpose is an adversary of God, and He only will see about and rectify that. If the hindrance is within, He will cleanse that, if you are willing. Have faith (complete trust) in God.

Amen (Truly, so be it).

www.ingramcontent.com/pod-product-compliance
Lightning Source LLC
Chambersburg PA
CBHW072103290426
44110CB00014B/1800